The Ten Lesson

First Edition January 2014

Front Cover Design – Ken Steinnerd, www.kensteinnerd.com
Back Cover Design – Miqui Mendez,
www.southwestbymiqui.com

The author of this book does not dispense medical advice or prescribe or recommend the use of any technique as a form of treatment for physical or medical problems without the advice or consultation of a physician, either directly or indirectly. The intent of the author is to offer information of a general nature to help in your quest for emotional and spiritual well-being. In the event you use any of the information in this book for yourself, the author assumes no responsibility for your actions.

Published in the United States

ACKOWLEDGEMENTS

To God and my Guides who teach me, fill me with joy and give me the most incredible experiences.

To my parents, brothers, sisters-in-law and their families, especially Ken and Jana, who learned the lessons with me. My family fills my life with love, laughter and adventure. They have blessed my life and I love them all dearly.

To Dr. Carol J Collins of Meadowsview Counseling Center who has been my counselor and teacher and who has been there for me for every step of this journey of spiritual awakening and growth. She believed in me when I didn't believe in myself. There aren't enough words to thank her for the role she's played my life.

To my dear friend Benay Unger who has always listened without judgment. She has helped me with my life in so many ways and is the talented editor of this book. She brought harmony to this story.

To my friends, relatives, co-workers and all who have shaped my life.

I thank all of you for being a part of my life and for your support, encouragement, help, guidance, friendship and love. This couldn't be without any one of you.

We must become the change we want to see.
Mahatma Gandhi

THE TEN LESSONS OF HEALING

<u>Forward</u>

Not one of us in this experience of "living" is alone. We may or may not be surrounded by family, friends and co-workers; but we are surrounded by God and all those in spirit. They are always available to help us; although we're often unaware of their presence. We may come to know them by paying attention to the synchronicities in life and by allowing ourselves time to experience each of these lessons of healing. We can experience them if we choose to be open and live consciously.

Everything we experience in life is part of our learning. The next moment is always an adventure yet to unfold.

The ten lessons are channeled information from my guides, Siddhartha and Michael. Siddhartha spent ten weeks providing the lessons, one per week, and Michael ten months explaining the lessons. Channeling is the most incredible part of my life. I hear my guides/ teachers and at other times I hear those who have passed – who have returned to spirit. (Throughout this book, I will refer to my teachers, Siddhartha or Michael as "he," "they" or "them"). They have all told me many beautiful things. Gradually, I have come to realize that hearing and understanding is one level of learning and knowing is another. Although I usually understand what they have told me, I am only beginning to know it, to feel the meaning of their words and to have them become a part of me. It is only when they become a part of me that I can live them and be healed.

I work full time, so most of the information came to me on

weekends while I took walks at a nearby wildlife refuge. This quiet time in nature is when it seems easiest for me to hear and to listen. However they will persist and help me at other times as well, while I am working or even in the shower. When I don't hear them for awhile, I miss them very much.

Siddhartha told me the ten lessons of healing are about every aspect of our lives: physical, spiritual and mental. It is in writing and studying each lesson that I am finding the answers to my questions. In reading this, I hope you will find answers to some of your questions.

I have channeled messages for other people and it always amazes me that I took what the spirit was saying one way but when the recipient received the message it had an entirely different meaning to them. Perhaps the same will be true with their words here as well. We each interpret the lessons in our own way. We find meaning in them as they pertain to our own life experience.

Physical, mental or spiritual healing is most often a gradual process, but there are those who can experience instant healing. While I believe we are all capable of instant healing, generally we choose to learn in our own time and way. If you are like me – you may find that you'll repeat many of the lessons several times until you truly internalize their complete meanings. Even now I am still experiencing many of the lessons in order to achieve a place where I can remain healed. That is my goal for this life. The lessons often help me to understand my life and life in general. When I get discouraged or find life difficult I make myself calm down, step back and review the lessons with the goal of discovering which lesson I've been lax in living. When I realize which lesson needs attention it helps me to know how to get back on track.

I am frequently reminded that we learn to heal ourselves not as

4

we hear each lesson, but as we come to know each lesson. How many of our physical ailments are the results of our mental, emotional or spiritual anguish? How much can we bear before it results in infirmity? What will it take for us to recognize the truths of the Universe? As we learn, we awaken and hear more clearly, see more clearly and come to know our selves; thereby not only acknowledging, but taking ownership of our thoughts, feelings, emotions and physical condition. We begin to know what is important and what is an illusion of our own mind. By this I mean the conditions and/or situations we have created in our mind and especially the ones that don't exist anywhere other than in our thoughts. They may exist now only because we continue to feed the illusion.

Shortly after the lessons began, I asked Michael, "What is a "healed" person?"

His response, "One who lives with joy."

This was such a simple answer – five words. I want and choose to be healed.

The lessons began on a bright, warm and sunny day. He began by telling me that learning to heal is like building a home. You must have the land and in this metaphor the land is Love. Healing cannot begin where Love is not present. We can only build upon Love. With the second lesson, I learned that the metaphor would continue… we are to build a home and in building this home we experience more love, peace and joy. I recall that long ago I was told that Peace is the sum of love and gentleness. It certainly fits and yet I still find myself continuing to contemplate that definition after all this time.

I wondered why he didn't spend time discussing the land we're building upon. He told me, "Child, without the land – nothing can be built. Without Love, healing is impossible. This is the very essence of all life. It is when we forget the lessons that our homes begin to crumble and to heal we must return to Love. When we learn, then we can build again and by having learned we build a home to endure all challenges and withstand the tests of time. Unless you have some knowledge and understanding of Love, you will not be able to build anything that will endure – and you will continue to suffer. It is this suffering that calls you to look within or as some say to look beyond the physical for consolation and answers. The answer is Love. Once you accept this then you begin to see the light and to learn. You then begin to become "more" of what you choose to be. Life and living has more meaning. There are fewer boundaries and life becomes both simpler and more complex. There is a yin and yang to all life. It is only complex in the respect that everything in life seems like a puzzle where you are looking for the next piece and to see how it fits in your life. There is a new perspective because Love is not only the source of life, but of learning.

Michael told me, "It's not about having things, doing things and going places. Although you are here to experience life and to live life joyfully and for many that includes living comfortably, acquiring things of beauty and seeing the world; it is about learning to Love. Not learning to say 'I love you,' but learning to be an example of Love by your thoughts, words and actions. It is learning how to receive Love – to know that you are always loved and to learn to share your Love with all who come into your life."

It seems to me that this is sometimes hardest to do with those with whom we share the most time. We take Love for granted. We lose our awareness of it. It is not part of our NOW until something threatens our comfort level. Michael replied to my thought, "You can take my Love for granted – know that it is always with you and that I am a part of you. When you truly know this then Love will never be a chore, anger will cease to exist as well jealousy, hatred, despair, doubt and fear; for I am the life. I am the light. I am the essence of All and that essence is Love. When you live the truth – Love is all there is and anything else is your illusion."

I had been reading a book from the 1950's to teach me more about love. In this book the readers are encouraged to use affirmations. The examples begin with, "Divine Love". "Divine love is healing my relationship with _____." "Divine Love is healing me so that I might accept abundance and prosperity." "Divine Love is healing my workplace so that all might find joy and success in their work." I started saying about four different affirmations daily and at night before I went to sleep. It helped immediately. I felt better and everything was going better at work and at home. I wanted more and one day while driving home, I thought why not create an affirmation to "awaken or become enlightened" and I was struggling to come up with a sentence that made sense. I was at it about ten minutes and finally asked Michael if he would tell me a good affirmation for this goal. My mind kept racing to create an affirmation and I didn't give him a chance to speak. Realizing that, I asked again and was told, the affirmation would be, "I AM DIVINE LOVE."

Lesson 1

These lessons came at a time when my brother and I were spending a little time each day channeling energy to several people with illnesses. To channel energy we simply connect with our mind and heart, our spiritual being to God and then visualize this energy flowing through us to whoever is in need of help. We simply view this as another form of prayer. Our objective is that the light (love) is healing this individual. This too is something I like to do at the refuge. Sometimes I ask for help from my Guide and he will instruct or give encouragement.

On this particular day, I asked if he would help me to do some energy work and Siddhartha told me he would tell me the "Ten Lessons of Healing". He said I will be given one lesson per week and during that week I would experience examples of the lesson. I had no idea what the lessons might be but I was surprised and excited by this news. Immediately I wondered whether this would really happen or if it was my imagination. I had only completed my thought when I heard, "Lesson one is Faith. Faith is the foundation for all the lessons, just as you have a foundation for your home." The foundation for this home can expand and contract depending upon on my Faith. He let me know that the foundation is an integral part of the home, since the rest of the home can only be built as strong as the foundation. He encouraged me to make my home strong and steadfast.

Like everyone I had a basic understanding of Faith. But I still didn't "feel" like I knew what Faith really means. When I asked friends and family for their definition of faith, I heard: "Faith is Trust." "Faith is that all this is real." "Faith is belief in God." "Faith is to believe in what cannot be substantiated." "Faith is to know you can always accept and tell the truth."

To understand the lesson, I had to be sure I understood the meaning of the word faith. The more I thought about it, the less confident I became. Although I had asked others what Faith meant to them, the real question was what does the word faith means to me? Upon reflection, my first thought was that faith means not having to be afraid. That surprised me. I remembered that for many years, often I heard my Guides say, "Don't be afraid." Frequently this was the only sentence I heard and generally when I was not aware of feeling afraid. On some occasions I would respond that I'm not afraid and he simply repeated the words: "Don't be afraid." I'm sure I have heard those words hundreds if not thousands of times and I didn't understand for years. I could be doing anything or be anywhere and suddenly hear, "Don't be afraid." It took me so long to realize that I have (or hopefully had) so many fears that I was not really conscious of them. It was my view of life. Occasionally I still hear, "Do not be afraid."

I know now that I've been afraid. I have been afraid of so much for so long; afraid of failure, afraid of being different, afraid of not being loved, afraid of not being good enough at my work, afraid of making big mistakes as a channel, employee or even as a sister, daughter or friend. I have been afraid of not being successful, afraid of losing those I love, afraid of being alone, of not having enough money, afraid of not being able to make other people happy and afraid of death. I am sure I could keep adding to the list. There are so many things I have feared in everyday life. I can call it worry or I can admit I am or have been afraid.

Before these ten lessons, I would have told you that I am a strong person and not afraid of much though I had the same "worries" anyone else does: paying the bills, job security, having money for retirement and so forth. I thought I was a person of little fear, because I have gone repelling, jumped out of an airplane, gone white water rafting and canoeing among other things that I thought proved that I had guts. I thought my fears never or rarely paralyzed my actions or activities. I had to look closely and see that there were many things I didn't do or attempt because of a lack of confidence or more accurately fear. I've avoided relationships for fear of being hurt or of not being able to find someone who could love me. I didn't change jobs for a long time for fear of not finding something better. I think Faith is one of my biggest lessons for this life.

It was time to ask myself what are the things I have always wanted to do but haven't and why.

I am learning to recognize that the worries, concerns and limitations I place upon my life are because of fear or lack of Faith. I'll even admit that my writing this had been a great fear. When this first began, every week I worried whether I would really hear the next lesson. Would I get it right? Worrying and showing my concern by worrying grew even as I was achieving some of my life goals. I began to not only wonder, but worry about what happens next? Isn't there more than this? Five days a week I go to work and do the daily chores that the average person does and yet for much of my life there has been a feeling of something missing. I often asked myself, "Where is my life going? What is the purpose of my life?" I worried about my life and my future. Living with fear was my normal state, from worrying about grades and friends as a child, to work, family and finances as an adult.

Along the way I finally realized that the word worry is another word for fear. So then I became "concerned". I spent several more years being "concerned" until I wised up and realized that I can give it different names – but it *feels* the same. I can call it by any name, but the feeling is fear.

To learn this lesson, I truly must change how I think so that I can change how I feel. I'm tired of feeling afraid. As a child I witnessed the tremendous Faith of my parents. Their lives were focused on family and work but it was their religious Faith that seemed to be the core of their being. It never wavered. They tried to teach their children how to be good people and they taught us to believe in God and prayer. As we grew up, they also taught me that worrying about someone is how you show you care about them. That was a major function of my parents, particularly my Mother. If you care about someone you worry about them and then of course you let them know – so they can be sure to feel guilty – whether or not they've done anything to warrant that worry. Worrying, is a learned behavior that is a tremendous waste of energy. It changes everything – it makes me miserable and I create more misery for myself and those around me.

But then I would think when a parent worries when a child is sick or hurt or when   I worry when my elderly mother doesn't answer the phone, isn't that the appropriate response in such cases? Immediately Michael spoke, "Child it (worry) is still a waste of energy. What a sick or injured child needs is love and care. Worry will not heal nor help the child or parent. A parent may show love or fear. Which do you think will help the child more? Is this not another example of Faith as we discuss the Ten Lessons of Healing?"

It seems that for me to understand Faith and to let it grow within me, I had to get rid of the weak foundation that I've been building upon for years: fear. Sometimes I found being a person of Faith difficult because I felt lost. What is my purpose? With lots of help, I have learned and come to believe that life is about Love. That for me the greatest purpose I can have is learning to live with love and to show my love for myself, others and the Source of Love - by any one of the names of God, and to love without judgment. Marianne Williamson explains this beautifully in her book <u>Return to Love</u>. "When we know that the Universe is love, then we can let go of the fears that come with guilt, shame as well as all those other thoughts and feelings of fear."

Since lesson one is Faith and the foundation for my home – then it makes sense that I want the foundation for my home to be based on Love. I remembered what Siddhartha said the first day, "Love is the land". I want to have Faith in a loving God. When I accept that lesson one is Faith, then I can understand that Faith is the foundation and Love is the firm, solid ground it is built upon. We need Love in our lives. I'm told this is the one thing we can all take for granted. We are all loved unconditionally. Within each of us is the essence of Love. In some beings this Love is a small spark waiting to ignite. In others the flame shines brightly. But it is within all of us and in everything.

Faith is living without fear. Faith is knowing that God / Universe will guide and provide for each of us. There is no such thing as failure as we are here to learn.

In the beginning, I could know and rely on my Faith for short periods. As my Faith grows, fear becomes less and less a part of my life. In learning about Faith, I began to understand the need for balance in my life. It allows me to appreciate everything in my life and to get the most from each day. I find it fascinating to see if I can figure out the meaning behind the synchronicities in my life and to see them as opportunities for learning. So many times I have been instructed by my friend and mentor Dr. Collins that everything happens for a reason.

As the lesson on faith continued, I began to wonder how it differed in meaning from: trust or "to know" and/or "to believe". Michael said, "Faith is to know that a being or their ability or concept is real, without doubt even when there is no data to satisfy the mind." He then asked me, "Do you know God? Do you know and have Faith in the Power of God? Do you have Faith in His Love and Goodness? Faith is all encompassing."

While on another walk he explained that to "believe" is to accept with more certainty than doubt…but doubt exists. Trust can only exist when there is an element of Faith. Trust is to rely or depend upon another. Trust is to know that one's actions are borne of love or goodness.

On a later walk he told me, "Faith is to know that God's love is in everything. Knowing is feeling this in your heart and mind. Believing is accepting with one's mind only."

He spoke briefly saying, "Mankind as a whole doesn't have Faith or trust in one another." Then this would mean that we doubt one another and that we do not know that man's actions are of Love. I would have to say outside my own circle of family and friends, it's true for me. These lessons are for us to learn so that this may change.

Healing begins when we begin to let go of fear. We know there is Love and we have Faith in God - the Universe and in our selves.

An employee once told me a one sentence prayer that I frequently repeat. I was told that it comes from AA. The prayer is, "God take away my fear and direct my attention to what you will have me be." That has helped me on some rough days at work. Lying in bed one night after having begun work on this book, I recited that prayer and felt that it was time to truly relinquish a particularly difficult financial situation to God. I've been trying to control things that I can't control and then I become worried and afraid. I keep repeating this lesson. But I can't seem to let go of the fear. Saying it and wanting it to go – doesn't make it go away.

Since 2007 I have owned my own business. Within a year of purchasing it the news was all about the price of gas, recession, inflation, healthcare, the housing market, credit, the war in Iraq and the declining state of our economy. Not a great time to be in a new manufacturing business that is tied to housing. My Faith got tested every time I listened to the news or on days when few orders came in. Michael asked why I was afraid when I've been repeatedly told my business will be fine. My fear on this subject has been declining for the most part, but sometimes fear creeps in that makes it hard to fall asleep at night or I can feel the stress in my gut. I've gone from constant fear to occasional fear that lasts a few hours. My Faith is growing stronger. I don't understand why I take such baby steps – when I have received so much encouragement and so much evidence of their love. It is a big lesson for me in this life.

In my mind, I told God that I give it all to him and I have faith that He will guide and protect me. Michael spoke to me and said very kindly, "You trust God, Mary. You don't have Faith. This is a start though. It's a good start…begin with trust and learn to have Faith"

I said, "I just don't get it. What is the difference – can you give me an example or something so I can understand?"

He answered, "Trust is like being 'in like' and Faith is being 'in love'." I understood and it felt different - this was something I could connect to and build upon. It feels right, but I'm not absolutely sure, but I want to hold on to this feeling.   I know now that trust is the seed of Faith. It is there waiting to grow within me.

With their teaching I have progressed through the past year. Where I would not have slept at night and been a mess all day with butterflies in my stomach and "stressed" to the max, now I sleep through the night and do not spend an hour trying to clear my mind to fall asleep.

Recently Michael has asked me to spend at least one-half hour working on this book every day and I've agreed to it and for the most part have done it. One day, I was working in the factory, when I found myself in a conversation with God. Now I talk to God pretty often, but it's not often that I hear Him or believe I heard him speak to me. He has a wonderful sense of humor. As is usual of late, I was thinking and worrying about the business. It is hard not to as there are times I have wondered how long I can keep the doors open. Yet I've learned enough to know that "worry" doesn't solve anything and I am aware of my struggle to learn Faith and know this is another opportunity to learn.

God said to me, "I'll take care of your business and you take care of my book."

 I quickly said, "It's a deal."

A few days later, I was working in the assembly area of the factory thinking once again about trusting and I could feel my fear ebb. Suddenly I actually knew and felt that Faith is the act of surrendering to God. The more I got used to the idea of trusting God, the more willing I became to just turn it all over to him.   At this realization I heard, "Yes, Child". Faith is not just letting go of the fear and worry – but that step of

15

surrendering to God. It has taken me years to understand that. I think perhaps it is not something you can really read about to understand, the feeling is one that must be experienced. It is healing.

DON'T BE AFRAID.

With each lesson, I was told that in the week following I would experience examples of what I was learning. This time it was Faith. The following were the some of the examples I experienced.

1) My Mother was reading one of Sylvia Brown's books about Angels and she told me that in the book Sylvia Brown gave an example that never fails: Ask your Archangels to have a particular person give you a phone call. The book states that you should to be sure to thank your Archangels after the call and that they don't mind you testing them in this manner. She told me that she had asked the Archangels to have a former co-worker call her; a woman she had not spoken to in nearly a year but with whom she would like the opportunity to visit. Mom knew that this friend was generally busy with her family and wasn't comfortable calling her. Her friend called less than 24 hours later.

2) My brother Ken and I had been channeling healing energy for several weeks to a client of Dr. Collins. We were anxious to know her progress. Together, we asked the Archangels to have Dr. Collins call with an update. The next day she called to give us a report.

3) The theme "Faith" seemed to show up in unexpected ways. The evening I was told the first lesson I was watching a rerun of the old Andy Griffith show. In this episode, Andy was having trouble believing his son even though his son was insisting that he wasn't lying to his father. The story was very

difficult to believe the way the child told it, but Andy decided he had faith in his son. In the TV episode he told the others, "Faith is trusting even when it is hard to trust, but you do it because you believe in the person."

4) Sometime that week, I also caught the end of a movie I had seen before called, "Joshua". The whole movie touches on love and faith.

5) Ken and I were talking one evening and I was telling him that I felt guilty about not working on "the book". But after I spent ten hours at work each day sitting at a desk working on my computer I find it very hard to come home and spend more time sitting at a desk. I often wonder whether the idea of my writing a book is realistic. While on the phone with Ken I said, "Be my witness that here and now I am asking the angels that if they really want me to write a book to help me win $1000 when I go to Nassau for my upcoming trip so I can buy a lap top computer. That way I could write anywhere I chose. Better yet, I'd like to win $2000 so that it would pay for the trip too." Sunday evening a friend and I were at a casino for dinner and a little gambling. We had agreed to stay another forty-five minutes and then return to our hotel to pack for our return flight the next morning. About thirty minutes later, I was playing a nickel slot machine when I won $2000.40. I wasn't even playing the maximum bet. When I saw the amount won, my first thought was of that phone call and request to the angels. And then I thanked them.

6) Driving down the road north of town I saw skywriting that said: U + God = Happy face.

I was determined to complete this book. The lessons are often in my mind and I am making progress to keep them part of my everyday life. Many things occur to remind me of the lessons and I see them showing up in different forms. I see how God is bringing these lessons through other people and other activities to my life and to everyone's. The teachers are out there. Now it's time to bring these lessons to you.

Lesson 2

It was the weekend after hearing lesson one. I was quite nervous. Would I really hear the second lesson? After all I was still struggling with my lesson on Faith. Nonetheless, it didn't take long before I heard, "Intention is the second lesson."

Siddhartha again compared healing to building a house. Having land to build upon is the first step and this land is Love. We lay the foundation and that is our Faith. Before we begin construction we need the design and that is Intention. It is our thoughts that determine the design and shape of what we build in our lives. He told me to remember: All, Aware, Ask, Act, and Allow. These are the five A's of Intention.

I asked Siddhartha to explain Intention and he replied, "It is all our creative thoughts. We are to be aware of each intention – every thought. It is our initial thoughts that are often the most powerful, because of the emotion behind them. There are two creative forces at work: thought and emotion. A part of Intention is to ask to know whether it is for our highest good and for help with our plans from God / the Universe. Once asked then we are to act, doing what we are able to do to fulfill our intention. Lastly, we allow our intention to come to fruition."

I recall that one of the first things Dr. Collins taught me over ten years ago, and has reminded me of several times since, is to change the way I think. All the lessons are simple concepts, but I realize that our understanding changes and broadens as we continue to learn and grow. She said I will be much happier once I change the way I am thinking. My never ending

19

"homework" is to keep my thoughts and expectations positive. For a long time I wasn't convinced, but I've come to know through experience that it's true. Sometimes I am not the best student. Although I understand and believe this, it has taken me a long time, to internalize it, to change my perception of "reality", particularly in certain areas of my life. Yet many times I have seen that when I changed my thinking, my life has changed.

When I am making an effort to be aware of my thoughts, I find that I can actually stop before a negative thought is completed. There is a flash of insight and I realize this isn't for my highest good, nor is it good for anyone else. Too often my thoughts are feeding my doubts or my fears, or are simply unkind. Being aware of our thoughts and the direction they are taking, is a learned behavior, one to be practiced until it is as much a part of us as getting dressed in the morning.

It amazes me how quickly I can change my feelings towards a person by changing my thoughts. By choosing what I think and feel about myself and others, I can change my attitude. It can take very little time before my feelings are aligned with my new thoughts. I am learning to realize that at any time I can change my expectations, hopes and dreams and above all my present. I decide whether to be positive or negative, happy or sad, angry or friendly and so forth. Though, sometimes I forget that this **is** my choice. Generally, when my foundation (my Faith) begins to crumble, I make a thousand "Design" changes.

Learning about Intention has made me more aware that many of our habits are acquired as children including our views of life. Among the things I learned as a child was to be "practical and realistic." While this perspective got me pretty far in life and was not necessarily a bad thing, it was, I now understand, a perception that was highly limiting. But with help I have learned there are positive and creative ways to get beyond the "realities" I was facing. I placed more limitations on my life than anyone had placed on me. In working to change this I have seen more opportunities in my life and I "intend" to turn my life into one of greater happiness, abundance and success. Again, I can change my reality with my thoughts and actions. I can change my Intentions. I am the only one who can change my goals, plans, objectives, all of which are synonyms for Intention.

One day while on the lesson of Intention, I was driving home from a walk at the refuge when Michael asked me to hold out my hand. I took my right hand off the steering wheel and turned it palm up. He said, "In your hand you hold all your life's dreams, hopes and desires. What shall you do?" Immediately I closed my hand tight to hold onto my dreams. At that moment, it felt as if that was all I had and if I didn't hold them I'd lose them.

A few moments later, I heard him say, "Wouldn't it be better if you let them go?" He suggested I simply blow them away and immediately I understood that I was holding them back instead of allowing them the freedom to create. I was trying to hold on to my dreams instead of allowing the dreams to happen. I lightly blew them off the palm of my hand and I heard him say, "Doesn't it feel better to have let that burden go and to give it to us…to the Universe?" It did and then there was/is hope for my dreams to come true.

He spoke again and asked, "What if I place a seed in your palm?" Suddenly an image of a sunflower seed in my palm popped into my head. He said, "It will not grow if you hold it in your hand." I knew I must prepare the soil and place in the earth. Tend to it and allow it to grow. It will never grow until we let it go to be planted.

My guides have made it very clear to me that while we hear and learn about all the lessons each lesson is built upon the previous lesson. I admit I haven't been a very good creator or more accurately at times in my life I haven't been the most positive creator. Instead of focusing on what I can accomplish, sometimes I focus too much energy on what I think I cannot do and, like all self-fulfilling prophecies, the result, of course is, that I can't. That is when my faith diminishes and fear reigns. Becoming aware of what we are creating is an important part of the lesson of Intention. Develop a strong foundation of faith and positive creative thoughts about everything in life. Spending more time focused on the good things in life is always more fun and yields more positive results in one's life. Understanding is one thing and practicing or incorporating the lessons into daily life is another. It sounds so easy and yet it requires continual effort as part of an ongoing process.

We spend our life learning and re-learning. Another important lesson for me was acknowledging my "Poor Me" syndrome. In the "Celestine Prophecy," James Redfield describes four types of personalities. They are the "Poor Me" – or the victim, the "Aloof" who tends to make people work to get any information including that which is generally volunteered; the "Interrogator "and, lastly is the "Intimidator" both pretty self-explanatory.

As part of this lesson I am learning to recognize myself in the people who surround me – both the positive and the negative. As Dr. Collins has informed me so many times, everyone is in your life for a reason. She also taught me that it is often the traits in others that annoy me, that serve as a mirror, meaning that I see the traits in them that I don't like within myself. Although I recognized this trait when I read Redfield's book – it wasn't until someone took an active role in my daily life that I became acutely aware of what I sound like when I (all too often) speak as if I am the victim of life. It's not an attractive trait and certainly not one I wish to continue. I wasn't sure why this is part of Intention so I asked. I was told that a major part of healing is to acknowledge who we are as well as to design the person we wish to become. It is much more about becoming an aware being of love and light. What is our Intention for our Body, Mind and Spirit?

I choose to be a spiritual being with an Intention to reach enlightenment and to live with joy. In learning this lesson it is easy to focus my intentions towards abundance and success and to look for positive results, but I need to be mindful of my spiritual growth as well.

I will admit that I'm not always the most upbeat. I am improving, because I choose to be happy. Sometimes it takes effort to think only happy thoughts. Why is that? Why would anyone choose to think unhappy thoughts? A friend recently told me that they heard on the radio that most successful people are optimists. They believe in their success and they are successful. It is time we think about what we are creating in our life and those about us. Sometimes I just sit and listen to the people around me discussing world or local or personal events and too often it is really sad to hear what they are creating with their wishes and opinions. This makes me more aware of my own thoughts. Perhaps by focusing on the positive in my life I can begin to improve the thoughts and views of those who surround me.

Michael explained that all thought is energy and every thought is creative energy. Your first thoughts on a subject tend to be the most creative as they tend to include substantial emotional energy as well. Therefore it is important to be conscious of the thoughts that we are sending out into the Universe. Once more I am reminded of what Dr. Collins taught me when I first saw her. I was really dwelling on all the rotten things that had been happening in my life and I told her rather sarcastically that I just can't wait to see what the next crummy thing will be. She told me if that is what I was expecting, I would probably get it. It was time for me to change the way I was thinking. I only stood to gain by trying it and she was right. Things started getting better quickly.

The lesson here is to know that our intentions are creating change in our lives and in others. Our intentions are not only for ourselves but for others too. Prayer is a powerful example of Intention. It is a time when we are aware of all our thoughts. Prayer is both an act and the asking of help for oneself or another and then we keep Faith to allow God / the Universe to respond. Perhaps that is why we often hear of "The Power of Prayer." We are using our thoughts and love to help another.

I have spent years thinking the lesson of Intention was teaching me to be aware and control my thoughts. It's really only the beginning concept of the Lesson of Intention. Intention is to teach us the fundamentals or the first step to create with God / the Universe. All thoughts and emotions are powerful creative forces which above all carry intent. I failed to understand the meaning of the word "Intention" which is defined by such words as aim, goal, target, objective and plan. It is not simply about controlling my thoughts and thinking positively, but that each thought is a fundamental part of the creative process. Every thought, emotion, spoken or written word is an Intention – it is an <u>act</u> towards a goal or objective. It is the plan or "design" for that which we choose to achieve.

These are all actions – all forms of energy. Remember there is "cause and effect" or what others might call karma. Others might even consider Newton's third law of Motion: For every action, there is an equal and opposite reaction. I asked for help wanting to know whether this applies to the spiritual realm as well and heard, "Yes Child, in that for every positive thought, it is an objective sent, one negative thought is overcome." I wasn't satisfied with is response. It wasn't enough to me that the opposite reaction is that part of the opposing or negative barrier is eliminated. He said, "Let's imagine that with every positive thought about your house you place a brick in the foundation. When you change your thought about what you wish it to look like, you move the brick to another location. When your thoughts are consistent, you keep adding bricks and eventually your house is built. When your thought is that this house will never get built, a brick is removed. Some are forever moving their bricks around and some destroy their bricks, give them away or let them be idle. Does this help you to understand?"

I have an Intention to have a beautiful flower garden. I can imagine it as I wish it to be. I cultivate the soil, plant seeds, tend to it. Yet I keep getting a mental image of a dandelion in different settings and sometimes there are bees flying in and about the dandelion. One minute I'm sure it will be beautiful and just as I pictured it, then I begin to doubt whether the seeds will germinate, whether the soil is right and the overwhelming work it will take to get it to be just right. Although I've done everything to create a beautiful garden, with each negative thought, with each moment of fear, it is as if I planted a weed or a dandelion. Unless I change my thinking to nurture the flowers, the dandelions of doubt will multiply and choke my garden.

When we change our thinking these negatives become

positives. I can see a bee moving from the dandelions to the fruit trees, pollinating them so they will bear fruit. I am reminded that the dandelion has medicinal value too.

Intention is about choices, conscious decisions. Our thoughts and goals are our choices.

In the present economic conditions and owning a fledgling business, I am out of necessity learning to control my thoughts and to maintain a positive outlook rather than one of doom and gloom. I believe that it is for this reason, that the doors of my company have remained open. This is an aspect of intention that for many months has never ventured far from my thoughts.

Often as I write in the evening or think of intention during the day, I ponder the meaning of this lesson. I felt as if I still wasn't grasping the heart of this lesson and then one evening the light came on. The "design" aspect is not about the conditions of my life, but the inner me. I am creating and choosing with each thought, word and action who I AM.

Is my intention to design myself in the image of God? This is about who I choose to become and whether I choose to learn to live with joy. By my thoughts, words and actions do I choose to heal, to live with light? What are my deepest goals? Are they to be a light worker, to be loving, to have a sense of humor, to be successful, to share? If I can be any type of person I wish to be, what shall I be?

It seems to me that the true lesson of intention is that we are creating and re-creating the person we are with each thought, with what we ask for, with our actions, what we permit to come into our lives and whether we actually have faith enough to allow God to lead.

Until I experienced a time of faith – it was all wishful thinking and sometimes hope. There was/is a belief that God was with me and there was peace, serenity, strength and comfort. Once I surrendered to God. I knew it was in his hands and then I could focus on the five A's of Intention…and build upon Faith. There are still times when my faith wavers but it is less fearful and each time the duration is shorter. Soon my trust and faith will be a strong and solid foundation. I AM building a new me – a healed me and a new life.

Basically I had the same experience every day the week I learned lesson 2. One of the first things I do when I come home from work is turn the television on…sometimes I sit down and watch it for a little while before I make dinner or I just listen as I read the mail etc. I have cable TV and consequently about four public TV stations. Every single evening, and once in the morning that week, when I turned on the TV I found Wayne Dyer talking about his book, "The Power of Intention." Mr. Dyer knows the importance and "Power of Intention" much better than I. Just to add to the intrigue, each time I turned the television on – the show was at the exact same place even though I was switching to a different station than the day before.

For the last year at work, my thoughts had been that we will make enough money to at least get by – meaning we'll be able to pay the bills etc. That's exactly what I'd gotten.

My Intention on January 25, 2009 was that by March 6, 2009 my company would be current on paying its bills. This means our quotes, orders and cash flow had to be bountiful to achieve this Intention. My new faith and positive attitude told me that there are no limitations, so my goals would be easily achievable. I'm happy to report that the company achieved that goal.

I know that I have heard promises from God. Among these promises, I have been told that He'll take care of my company – that I have nothing to fear. In some of my more "clear moments" I'm able to see how my thinking, my words and even in my actions I have gotten in the way of "receiving" the fulfillment of His promise. My own doubts and fears have prevented this from culminating in success. I was told the worst of my hard times were over in 1993 and yet I still doubted. Michael has told me it (the business) will be successful. And I've noticed that when I consciously change my intentions the business does better. As I've said before, this lesson learning is an ongoing process.

Lesson 3

It was another Saturday and I was still nervous as I wondered if I would hear the next lesson. It was shortly after I arrived at the refuge that I heard Siddhartha saying "Unity, Unified, United". Then he said that he wanted one word to describe this lesson… let it be "Unification". He told me to realize what all the forms of this word mean in our life. I thought of unions - both as marriage and work. That we live in the United States. The names of Churches including "The United Church of Christ", "Unity Church" and there are several others. He told me to think of what each of these mean. I asked for more and he told me he wanted my brother Ken and me to study and he would give us more tomorrow.

I studied. Although I know the meaning of the word, I looked up the definition in The Merriam-Webster Dictionary, "To make into a unit or <u>coherent whole</u>." One of the first things that both Ken and I thought of when we heard this was Einstein's Unified Field Theory although I certainly didn't understand it. I found myself reading about it and Einstein's theory of relativity and some of the very basics of Quantum Physics, the latest string theory, etc. The most elemental concept of the Unified Field Theory, in respect to string theory, is that the Universe is composed of ten dimensions and within those ten dimensions everything in the universe can be broken down and composed of loops of vibrating strings. Often in "New Age" philosophies you hear of vibrations and strings or cords connecting us to one another. I don't know if it is the same, but it is plausible. Now scientists are investigating whether there are more dimensions within the strings themselves. It would seem that they are gaining ground on developing an actual mathematical equation to express the Unified Field Theory and to "prove" that we are all connected.

Having read what I did, it seemed obvious that Siddhartha wanted us to understand that we are all composed of energy and that we are all connected. We are connected to all that is - to the source, God, nature and to one another.

The following day I went to the refuge and asked if we were on the right track. He said we were and that the only thing he would add is that we are not experiencing unification when we feel separate or alone. He also suggested we think of this both as if we are the one being healed and as one channeling energy to another as being the same. We are all connected to make one coherent whole, so that when we help to heal ourselves or another we are simply raising the energy level of the whole. It makes sense then that when we help another we are also helping ourselves. When we understand Unification, we know that when we reach out to help each other we help to heal the whole universe. Again, every act of helping another is not only helping one individual – but the whole. It sounds so simplistic and yet it is mind boggling to think of the ramifications if we could all learn to help each other. The power we have as a unified group to change everything in our lives – to change our existence.

So when we ask "is this for my highest good and the highest good of the Universe" we are asking a significant question. In answer to this question Siddhartha said, "Child whatever is for your highest good is for the highest good of the universe?" Posing such a question in its current form is to acknowledge awareness that we are unified.

I asked how this worked into the building of the house. He began at the beginning.... Love is the land on which you build your foundation of Faith. Intention creates the design of our home and Unification will allow you to begin building. Know that all that is added will be connected and held strong. We are

30

not alone in the construction of our home. We not only have our physical crew, but a spiritual crew to help us build. Since we are all connected in every way – then it nearly goes without saying that there is divine assistance not only available, but willing and waiting to assist us in all that we do to build our homes.

"We are one Child in all we do and when we acknowledge this connection of love, then we can know another's Truth whether it be one of pain, love or joy." We all choose to share the greatest moments of our lives...the ones where we feel the most. Our thoughts and feelings transcend the physical dimension. All our thoughts, words and actions determine not only the design of our home, but how it comes together and the structural strength of it.

While considering all the implications of Unification, I thought about the statement that says, "We can only really heal ourselves" and I have decided that is not true. We are simply the only ones who can choose to heal or not to heal. I have come to understand that we are all connected to the source, but only when we truly believe we are all connected to one another does channeling take on another meaning as well, then you have multiple beings connected to the source and suddenly the energy is doubled, tripled, etc., by the number of those participating. We also consciously and unconsciously choose whether to accept channeled energy, including prayer, when we decide whether we are open to these concepts or lessons.

On several occasions Dr. Collins has talked to me about our connection to God – that this connection to the Universe can be metaphorically compared to a pipe. We all have a pipe that is connecting to the source of Divine energy. It is up to each of us whether we permit this energy to flow... Every home has the main valve...we can shut that off or leave it on to connect to the Source. She has told me that we can clench the pipe and close it with our thoughts. It is up to each of us to keep the pipe open. We are all connected – like pipes again, but just as each location has a separate shut off valve, we do the same with all those around us. We choose who we consciously allow into our lives and who we will shut out.

While I was walking at a wild life refuge, the day he was to tell me about this lesson, near the entrance I passed a bench. Sitting on the center of the bench was a rock about 1-1/2" in diameter. I noticed it, walked on by and didn't think anything more about it at the time. After Siddhartha had told me the third lesson and I was walking back towards my car, I sat down on the same bench to see if he had anything else to tell me. The stone was still there sitting in a tiny pile of sand. He told me, "This piece of rock is an example of unification. Just looking at it you can see that it a conglomeration of sand, shell and other elements... and yet it is a rock, an item of perceived strength – a coherent whole". It was easy to see that it is made of multiple unified particles that gave it strength. I was asked if this rock is separate. I knew what he was getting at; although it may have been lying on the bench it is still part of the earth. If I had seen on the ground, I would not have given it another thought. Sometimes we see ourselves as separate but this is only an illusion. Just like the rock we are all connected. Perhaps for some it may be easier to see the rock's connection to the earth than it is to see our connection to the earth and to the Universe.

During my walks at the refuge, it is not uncommon for me to become oblivious to the world about me. A few times I have nearly walked on wildlife – a snake or an alligator. When I suddenly become aware of their presence – there is an overwhelming sense of fear and both the animal and I react at the same time. They are always faster and thankfully head in the opposite direction. Each time this has happened I wonder how it is that these animals did not scatter or move until my brain sent thoughts of fear. Our movements were simultaneous...although I felt fear – there was still, what at the time seemed like eternity, a lapse waiting for my body to respond and run. There must be an energy connection that allowed them to sense my fear – my thoughts and feelings.

On numerous occasions Siddhartha and Michael have encouraged me to bring a camera. They want me to be aware of them, but also aware of all about me as I look for the perfect picture. One day I had a camera in my pocket and I saw how beautiful the refuge was. I took about a dozen pictures – I could see the beauty in my surrounding – in even the smallest objects. In those moments, I truly understood that God created all this about me. I am part of what God created. I am whole and I am a part of the "whole". These are no words to convey feelings that reach within and touch parts of me that had been hurt or sheltered to keep from being hurt. In this moment of realization, the feelings seemed to reach within and connect to my mind, body and soul. Emotions that were so strong I felt them physically in my chest and gut – a sense of wonder and awe.

As I was initially preparing to write this chapter, I went to the refuge. I had not reviewed the material in months – perhaps even a year. So I asked Michael, "What's the most important idea I was to convey about this lesson?" He repeated what he had told me the first time, that when we feel alone, we are not experiencing Unification. This is an easy way to identify that we have chosen to mentally disconnect or separate from the Source. We can change this by using the information from the first two lessons....change our thinking and to have faith.

In reviewing this I read again the definition from the dictionary and I understand it a little better. In Unification we know that we are "whole" when we are aware of our connection to the Universe to all that is around us seen and unseen. Physically we are connected with every breath we breathe, with the food we ate, the water we drink – with all that sustains our body. We are connected emotionally and mentally with every interaction we have with people or beings in our life. Beyond that with our very thoughts and feelings we are connected spiritually.

I'm sure that it was no coincidence that as I once again began working on the lesson of Unification a major event was taking place in my life. Shortly before her 86th birthday my Mother came to live with me. She needed assistance as her vascular dementia progressed. For a year and one-half she could essentially care for herself, but her ability to communicate had declined significantly. We were advised that she was in stage 3 of the 5 stages of dementia.

I asked Michael if he would tell me something that would help her memory. He gave me instructions using natural ingredients for which I absolutely had no experience, but within a few days I saw improvement. It helped for several months, but then there were other bouts of an illness which resulted in her missing doses of the suggested items and there was a substantial difference in her memory recall. When she resumed the homeopathic "medicines" there was improvement, but not back to where she had been before the illness.

This homeopathic treatment seemed to slow the dementia in addition to the medical prescriptions she had been on for some time. Yet, gradually her ability to recall names of people and the names of items diminished. She still knew the people or the items, but would be unable to come up with their names. That continued to be the case for a while. Then a few weeks later her ability to know what the item was when you mentioned its name began to decline.   Yet all this time she was cognizant of what was occurring and would say, "I only have the mind of a child" or "I don't have much of my mind left."

It was terribly frustrating, demoralizing and depressing for her. More and more often she would express a desire for her life to be over.

At that point I asked Michael for something that would help her to regain her ability to express her thoughts. I asked him if there was something that could do this and he said yes. I asked if it was something I could get and he said yes. This was when I was once again writing about the lesson of Faith… and still questioning.   Even after many, many years, sometimes it is still difficult for me to discern whether I "hear" them or if I'm really hearing me. This was one of those times and I wondered whether I was hearing "yes" because I wanted to hear yes.

The following weekend, I sat down to listen and see if Michael would tell me what would help my mother. I expected to hear a recipe for some kind of oils again. He told me he would have to spell it…. And I became anxious and nervous.
R A M A L ….. I don't know any word that begins like that and I had an image in my head of the letters and there was a L….Q U   S A.   Next I had an image of the ocean, but it didn't look anything like I had seen in Florida or on either coast.

Next I heard Cronwall or Cronwell. I was getting rather frustrated and wondering whether I was making it up. The image of the ocean – had a section of rocky coast and I could see small plants – lichen on the rocks. I could also see pasture or animals grazing.

I started googling what I had and moments later I had

Ramalena Siliquosa. I learned that lichen grew in England, Ireland and Scotland and that was an important factor. I searched for a few hours and found that although it grew there, it was not available in any form for sale.

I asked Michael again if there was something more readily available to give to my Mother that would help her and I could see a picture of letters in my mind. U   L   V   A and of course this didn't make any sense to me. I didn't know what to think and was about to give up and Michael said, "It will not be as good as the lichen, but it will have many of the same properties." This time I googled Ulva and was led to Ulva Lactuca and it is commonly found in the waters in the targeted area. Very quickly I learned that "Ulva Lactuca" is more commonly called Sea Lettuce.

At first I wondered why he simply didn't tell me Sea Lettuce, but I realized I would have stopped immediately with something along the East Coast of the US and probably not even listened for more information. After receiving such information I was compelled to read and study as much as I could and to ease my mind that I wasn't doing something that could harm my Mother. But mostly I did it because I didn't have the greatest confidence that I was actually channeling the information or making it up.

After searching I fell upon a source from Scotland. After exchanging a number of emails I ordered capsules. I also spent hours trying to learn about the nutritional, medical, and pharmaceutical properties of Ulva Lactuca. It seems there is little actual research on marine algae or sea lettuce. It has been used for years as food, spice and as an herbal remedy, but not for the purpose I intended. It did not appear that any harm could come from trying this and so I gave one tablet to my Mother at lunch time.

Saturday – no change

Sunday – no change

Monday – no change

Tuesday – more alert part of the time and heard a noun or two
that I wasn't sure was still part of her vocabulary. She seemed
more sure of who various family members and friends were at
least part of the time. I was actually discouraged and
despondent that I couldn't be certain of improvement.

Wednesday – Definitely signs of improvement. She spoke with
numerous sentences without searching for words. I heard her
say the words, coat, throat, floor, bathroom, linens, clothes,
cars. Not everything was referred to as "this, these or things".
She was able to recall and tell me some events of her day. She
remembered where articles were kept, that had previously been
forgotten. She remembered events from yesterday and one
from a week ago without any effort on my part to jog her
memory. She made phone calls to friends, whereas she usually
avoided calls or made them as short as possible.

Thursday – There were more full sentences that flowed with
ease and use of nouns instead of this, these or things. She
seemed so much more alert and interested in trying to express
herself as she was having more success. Often words flowed
as they would for anyone. She was interested in reading. Her
vocabulary improved tremendously.

Friday – She was talking much more. When I called her she
was able to tell me what she was doing. There was some
difficulty and yet she succeeded in finding the words. Again
there were nouns and adjectives I hadn't heard in months.
Naturally she was happier, but still reluctant to say she was
doing better….but I sensed hope. The changes I witnessed

were phenomenal – it was a miracle to me. There were moments I would forget she had a problem. It was exciting.

Saturday – Nearly all progress was gone, her ability to communicate was nearly to what it had been before the Sea Lettuce. It was discouraging. Was this really a two day miracle? I was nearly ready to abandon the idea of giving this to my Mom. Why have her taking all this stuff and giving her hope when it appeared to be unlikely that any long term benefit would result.

I kept searching the internet for any medical studies on Alzheimer's / Dementia and even went in chat rooms on this topic. There was an internet buzz about the possible benefits of curcumin. I eventually abandoned the sea lettuce and tried the curcumin, but the disease won. I often wonder what if I had increased the dosage on the sea lettuce if there would have been a more long term change, but I couldn't risk being the one to hurt her instead of helping her.

I love my Mother and I am certainly connected to her in many ways. It helps to know we are all connected and perhaps the greatest connection of all is love.

Still wanting an easier way to explain Unification, I asked Michael for examples over the next several days. I have to admit that even when some things happened, I wasn't aware until I looked back at the end of the day and thought it over. The following were examples of where I saw Unification in my life.

One evening, as I had promised, I did energy work on someone's husband. I don't know why but tears just ran down my face and I felt totally at peace. While channeling energy for this man I was connected to the greater Universe.

Another day while driving home from work, I heard a Carpenters song on the radio and that reminded of playing ping pong in a friends basement as a kid. The Carpenters album seemed to be playing every time we were down there talking and playing ping pong. We were friends since fourth grade, but had grown distant since I moved to Florida. We hadn't communicated in about six months but that night I got a long email from her. I might not have connected these two events if I hadn't been aware that Michael was trying to fulfill my request.

It took me quite a while to see that part of the lesson of Unification is also learning to work together with those around us to achieve a common goal. I realized this while watching a Cardinal baseball game. Any sport team must work as a cohesive unit to make it the playoffs and to win a championship.

When we work together to achieve a common goal - we are always stronger and usually take greater strides towards a successful outcome. It's about working together to achieve goals or fulfill our Intentions our life. Everyone around us can teach us and help us to grow and fulfill our Intentions. Through Unification we too learn our lessons for life.

Lesson 4

The following week I entered the refuge believing I would hear the fourth lesson. After three weeks, I began to believe in the process and that I wasn't making this up. I was fascinated and eager to learn the next lesson and anxious to see how it would show up in my life. A few minutes after I arrived I asked Siddhartha what the fourth lesson was. Instead of telling me, he answered with a question. "Think about the house analogy, what do you think the lesson is?" After thinking a moment I guessed that it was something comparable to financing or getting a loan to build. We have the land, the foundation and the plans. We also have connections and are united with all who will help us to build. How do we get the funds or what we need to actually the build the house?

Siddhartha told me to assume I had financing. He said, "There will always be financing whether we think we have good credit or bad credit. There is no interest and there are no penalties. It is never a problem for anyone to get the "backing" to heal. It is a given."

That assuring response made me think of the promises or the times I bartered with God to have something change in my life. Whether I had kept or broken promises that I made to Him, He is always there to help me heal. Then I heard, "Do you remember that even when you knew you had been approved for a home loan that you still had to get an appraisal?" It seemed almost a formality – a confirmation that the value of the property met or exceeded the loan amount. I remembered.

He told me, in this lesson I have to do my own appraisal. I have to know that I am worthy of healing. I have to know my own value. I have to look within and see whether I deem myself worthy of healing. Am I afraid to heal or afraid I can't heal? This requires a self-examination to see the limitations or conditions I have set on my ability to heal. There are times I have set constraints telling myself there is no way I can heal until I meet other conditions that I set. At times I am still surprised at how I have chosen to sabotage myself. All of these factors determine the value I place on my house and the amount of the gift. He told me what I am receiving is never a loan, but a gift. Even so, there is to be this step.

Through the years, Dr. Collins has told me, my brother Ken has told me and I have read, "**There are no mistakes – only experiences that are opportunities to learn.**" Repeatedly I hear these words or variations of them and for the most part, I've said, "Yes, I get it. I understand." But it didn't take on any personal meaning until Michael talked to me again. Until then I thought of it as more of an excuse to avoid responsibility or just a way to make someone feel better. Perhaps for the first time I accepted it as truth.

Many of the significant events in my life are experiences I view as "mistakes" and they seriously impact how I feel about myself. This is a major factor in my self evaluation.

When I sat down to write this book, I paused to think what it means to be healed. It must be important that I remember that a healed person is one who lives with joy…who knows joy. Michael said, "Yes Child. In that joy there is only love and light. Remember life is a circle. There are no endings Child…there is eternity and infinity. Only your experiences are finite and become memories to build upon as they have a hand in your learning. You are not the sum of your experiences Child. You are the sum of what you LEARN from your experiences. In some cases you may be the victim, in others the aggressor, others a witness but you learn from each experience. If it is only the event without the learning – then you shall repeat the lesson Child just as you do in your earth schools. You chose to learn, to grow in love and light. Sometimes you choose lessons which seem hard, because you remain caught in the experience rather than learning the lesson. That is why it seems so difficult. You become "caught" because you return to fear and/or your intentions are filled with fear and/or you work to separate yourself from all those to whom you are connected. While all the lessons are there for the learning, a home is construction from the earth up. Is that not so?"

Now I have begun to change my thinking and tell myself these are opportunities to learn. If I look within to see that these "mistakes" were events that changed my life and I did learn or am learning, then I quickly find that I feel differently about myself. I can stop regretting what I thought were mistakes and recognize them as valuable lessons that helped to shape my life and my being. I can see in these events a different lesson than I had years earlier – time has given me a new perspective. By accepting that there are no mistakes only opportunities to learn, I alter my perception of my life and my self-evaluation and in a much more positive and loving way.

I have also taken the opportunity to look closely at how this affects all aspects of healing. How often I don't take care of myself physically – because something else is more important or I don't think I can change or it's something that can wait until tomorrow. Tomorrow is one excuse I frequently use and that particular tomorrow, never seems to become today. Why do I procrastinate on healing or helping myself? Perhaps I doubt whether I can accomplish the goals I want to achieve or doubt my own skills or abilities. There are times when I look within and wonder am I even worthy to be receiving this information?

Self-examination is not a task I enjoy. I know there are limitations I have placed on my life in regard to healing as well as abundance. There are times I believe I can't achieve my goals or that I can't have what I desire until I meet some self-imposed goal. Thinking about this lesson for myself and for others close to me, I realize this is where many of us stop in the healing process. We have faith, intention and even unification - believe in our connections, but we lower the self-appraisal. Somehow we determine we are not worthy or it can't happen for me. Perhaps we've made too many mistakes and don't believe we're good enough. Other times we're afraid to take the chance. We might fail. We don't trust in our self or we have forgotten our Faith.

There are no mistakes – only experiences and opportunities to learn.

I asked Siddhartha "Is the fourth lesson appraisal?" It was a moment before he answered. He said the lesson is in accepting and recognizing your own self-worth and value. To do this you evaluate your own spirit, heart, and mind – your life. Lesson four is Evaluation…self-evaluation.

I know I have my own strengths and weaknesses. In writing this I am understanding even more how each of these lessons are connected and the things I can change about myself to make my life better and more joyful. There are simple things I can do to succeed and know happiness. In an ordinary day there are ways for us to heal emotionally, mentally and spiritually.

The day before I was to begin redrafting this lesson, I had an appointment with Dr. Collins. Last time I saw her, Michael intervened and asked her not to discuss whatever she had planned to discuss with me until the next time I saw her. I admit my curiosity was peaked. I was eager to see what it was all about. Now I knew I was going to begin re-writing this chapter, but she didn't. The topic of her discussion was basically all on this subject. The minute she began talking it was about whether I believed I was worthy to have my dreams come true… to have my "wants" become my "reality". Immediately I thought, "Wow, it's no coincidence that she is talking to me about this subject at this particular moment. It is my time to actualize this lesson and change my life.

As I was writing this lesson, I was still looking for more insight and asked Siddhartha and Michael for more information. They answered, "Child, you must know that you are loved no matter what you do or what you have done. This life is your opportunity to learn to love yourself and others. Knowing you are a person, a being of great value – knowing that you are worthy of all there is, knowing what is of value to you."

What is of value to me? Suddenly, I don't know the answer to that question and the first responses that I think of are all things that I have been afraid to let myself have in my life: Someone who cares about me, loves me; success without limitations; opportunities; to be a good channel. Then it struck me, I am worthy of my dreams becoming my reality.

"Yes child."

"And you would help me?"

"We are all connected Child. Would you not help those you love? Keep us connected and the light will shine for all through you."

The question isn't am I a good person or a bad person. But

rather am I a spiritual being growing in love and light? That's the heart of the matter. I have to make that decision and know the answer is true. It's time to get off the fence. Can I accept that there are no mistakes only experiences?

God thought I was worthy to be here. God knows our value is limitless as we are one. If we are connected with God, how can I be unworthy? How can anyone?

Having achieved this insight I again asked for more explanation about this lesson. Michael asked me if a child that makes mistakes is unworthy of the parent's love, friend's love – of anyone's love, much less God's love which is always a given? I answered a child's mistakes are part of the learning process. It is to be expected. They teach the child about right and wrong and more importantly that they are loved no matter what they do in life. Hopefully we will encourage all children to believe that they can achieve whatever they set out to achieve in this life. He responded, "We may be adults in the physical world, but we are children spiritually. So too are our mistakes expected and used to teach us that we are loved. God and all those in spirit would never consider us unworthy of love or God's bounty and all the bountifulness of our world."

A long time ago a man I dated told me I could never find the right person until I cared about myself. I keep thinking about that now. Perhaps I would not be overweight or single if I cared more about myself. But that is not the thought of someone who is worthy. And I AM worthy. I AM a good person. I AM a spiritual being. I AM deserving of good people and good things in my life. I AM worthy of abundance and prosperity. I AM worthy of success. I am connected to God and that alone makes me worthy.

I was lying in bed too awake to fall asleep and I asked Michael or God to talk to me about this lesson. Michael responded,

"Mary, aren't all these lessons based on love?"

"Yes."

"Then this lesson too is about love." A moment or two later it sunk in, the real heart of this lesson is, do I love myself?

Why is it that I had to think about the answer to my own question? It seems that my answer would be yes; I love myself simply for the reason that I am. Yet I grew up taking my cues about whether I was loveable from my parents, family and child hood friends. As I matured I found that my self-worth often depended on the how I compared myself to others. Therefore I was constantly **judging** everyone around me as well. Not realizing all of us are just here to learn.

"Child it is important to remember the lessons you have built upon. Knowing you are loved and worthy will allow the joy to begin to flow to you in ways you can know it and know that you a student progressing on your path. Remain steadfast to your faith, design and stay connected to the love and light in your life."

During the following week several events occurred that seemed directly connected to this lesson.

It was a "different" week. I experienced a number of physical problems that probably tied in some way. One morning I got up and I couldn't straighten my left leg. The muscle had tightened so much it had slipped off my knee and wouldn't allow me to straighten my leg. I had to get a pair of crutches and went to work on them that day. My boss set up an appointment that morning with a massage therapist who was able to relax the muscle and I was able to walk again. It was stress from what was going on in my life, particularly at work, and how I was choosing to handle various situations.

It was also the week during which my Mom, for the first time ever, asked me for a message from my Dad. She was feeling so bad. One evening she cried as she told me how she wished she had been a better wife. She blamed herself that she didn't realize he had some respiratory distress from second hand smoke. She wished she had been more than she had been. More in many ways. It was heartbreaking to listen and to hear her pain especially when I know my Father would never have agreed with what she was saying and in his message he told her so. It was easy to see that she was hurting from her view of herself. My Dad would have never blamed her for his choices.

I had the opportunity to purchase the company where I was employed and decided to discuss this with my former boss to get his opinion. Purchasing the business meant putting my home up as collateral for the loan. He considered all the pros and cons of my buying the company and kept asking me if this is really what I want. He said, "I don't think you realize that you will only succeed at what you really want to do. I believe you can do it but I'm not convinced this is what you really want."

During the week, I was given the following prayer:

Prosperity Prayer

I know that God is my source of all supply and riches. God's riches are unlimited and readily available to me.

I am divinely guided in all ways. Divine ideas come to me quickly, with ease and under grace for my highest good and the highest good of all concerned.

The life I live, services I render, work I do, products I create, bless and help humanity. I attract men and women who are spiritual, honest, loyal, faithful, talented, blessed with a sense

47

of humor, who contribute enthusiastically to the peace, prosperity, progress and success of my life, services I render, work I do, products I create.

I am an irresistible magnet to my good and attract fabulous wealth by giving the best of myself, services I render and products I create. I am constantly in tune with the wonder of God and the substance of wealth.

Divine intelligence governs all my plans and purposes. I know everything I need to know instantly. I predicate all my success on the truth that God leads, guides and governs me in all my undertakings.

There is serenity, security and peace that rules my life.

I am a tremendous success. I am one with God. God is always successful; therefore, I must succeed.

I radiate love and a sense of well-being to everyone I meet.

This includes those who surround me, my family, friends, fellow employees, those I hold near and dear to my heart.

God's love and wisdom fill my heart and mind with all I need to succeed, prosper and experience life to the fullest.

All the love, dynamic power, energy, inspiration, light, truth, creative ideas I need are mine.

There is no thing, no problem, no circumstance or situation that can withhold what is mine by right of consciousness. There is no delay in Divine Mind.

"...Be transformed by the renewing of your mind. Then you will be able to test and approve what God's will is. His good, pleasing and perfect will. His will for His beloved creation is always good." (Romans 12:2)

Lesson 5

I walked into the refuge this morning and Siddhartha asked me whether I accepted the first four lessons as truth. Did I believe them?

"Yes," I responded.

He said, **"Truth is the Fifth Lesson."**

I was hearing "truth" but found myself thinking "honesty". He told me quite clearly, "The lesson is not honesty but truth. There is a difference. In Lesson Four you learned the importance of Self-evaluation. Now you must discover if you can live life truthfully - accepting your own truths and the truths of others. Truth will be the floor upon which our house is built. Truth is of light only."

Immediately an image of a Ying Yang symbol came into my mind and I thought, "Then there is an opposite as well." He said, "Yes, there is an opposite - Falsehoods. They are of the dark. So therefore, Truth can only be light. Everything is to be built upon light." And I knew he was referring to our house.

I admitted to myself that I didn't know the difference between honesty and Truth, but I'd figure it out. So when I got home I went straight to the Merriam-Webster Dictionary:

> Main Entry: **truth**
> Pronunciation: 'trüth
> Function: *noun*
> Inflected Form(s): *plural* **truths** /'trü[th]z,
> 'trüths/

Etymology: Middle English *trewthe,* from Old English *trEowth* fidelity; akin to Old English *trEowe* faithful -- more at <u>TRUE</u>

1 a *archaic* : **<u>FIDELITY</u>**, **<u>CONSTANCY</u>** **b :** sincerity in action, character, and utterance
2 a (1) : the state of being the case : **<u>FACT</u>** (2) : the body of real things, events, and facts : **<u>ACTUALITY</u>** (3) *often capitalized* : a transcendent fundamental or spiritual reality **b :** a judgment, proposition, or idea that is true or accepted as true <*truths* of thermodynamics> **c :** the body of true statements and propositions

The morning I was to begin writing this lesson, Michael told me that beginning with the fifth lesson we determine the beauty and elegance of our home.

I asked, "So does it depend upon how truthful I am whether I would have dirt, wood or stone floor?"

He asked me, "How do you intend to live your life?"

"Truthfully," I answered.

"Then you forget the lesson of Unification – we are here to help you – to be your building crew. If your intention is to have a beautiful home, then we are there with only the best supplies. It would be your choice whether to cover it with dirt or to let it go to disrepair."

Michael said that without Truth communication does not exist. There is no real connection without Truth….nor strength. He explained that the floor must be Truth; that we can only build upon Truth. He also said that Truth is not just about speaking truthfully; it is about living one's Truth. This means that not only are my words to be of Truth, but my thoughts and actions as well. "We must be in total alignment with our thoughts, words and actions and in that there is power and strength. There is power – energy in all things and when these are all aligned (thoughts, words and actions) there is great power. Truth enhances our connection to all things and beings both in the spirit and the physical.

Hopefully with each of the remaining lessons, I am not going to have to experience illness of some kind, but during this week's lesson I had hives. It was itchy and uncomfortable. I spent several days trying to see how the lesson of Truth was showing up in my life. There were a few occasions when I was tempted to stretch the Truth or avoid responding altogether, but I didn't. In Louise L. Hay's book "Heal Your Body", she associates hives with "Small, hidden fears. Mountains out of molehills."

The most significant event taking place at that time in my life, was that I was deciding whether to purchase part of the company where I worked. It meant using a significant amount of the equity in my home for the purchase of the business. Frankly, I disliked the idea of potentially jeopardizing my home.

I kept wondering if it was my fear of doing this that caused the hives. But I have always dreamed of owning and operating my own business.

A week went by and I still didn't feel like I saw a lesson of Truth in my life beyond trying to figure out what I wanted to do. Did I want to buy this company or not? One day at work I was listening to two men tell me exactly what they thought of a co-worker. They were annoyed at this man and nothing they had to say was positive. I understood why they were irritated and while their feelings were honest I was thinking – you're only seeing one side of this man right now. You are too angry to remember or see his good points – what they were saying was not all true. Suddenly I got it…Truth. Their opinion of this man wasn't the whole truth.   When I'm judging others, how truthful am I?

Perhaps Truth is also about seeing clearly; not fearing what might happen or could happen. It's seeing people – myself and others, for who they are really are.   I was thinking about this as I walked at the refuge and Michael told me again that Truth is about <u>living your Truth</u>. He said, "Truth is not how others see you or what they have to say about you. You have to know your own Truth and live according to it. As you grow and live your Truth – your Truth may become more pure. You will understand this more as you experience it. Truth is to know yourself. You have experienced the lesson of Evaluation, where you have determined and know that you are worthy of healing, of knowledge and of love. What are your truths?

I thought it must be all the things where I felt total conviction. But Michael immediately said, "It is not about conviction. It is not about any word that begins with "con". What is the first part of that word?"

"Convict," I answered.

He said, "Do you think that relates to Truth?"

Later, I looked on the internet and one of the first definitions of conviction was to "persuade by argument." That doesn't sound like Truth to me.

He asked me again, "What truths do you live by? What are your truths?"

What is my own Truth? I pondered this for a long while. I want to live my life without regrets, but while I accept certain events in my life, I still regret several. I want others in my life, but I don't want them to make any demands on me or my time. I like to help people or do things for people when it suits me. I am successful. I am a good person. I can be a better person. I am light. I am love.

I am not better than anyone nor am I a lesser being. I do not have to work at making people like me; I need only to be at peace with myself and accepting of others for they too are learning the lessons – consciously or unconsciously.

A few days later I was talking to Michael again about this lesson. He said I can only know peace when I live and rest upon Truth.

So what is the one truth by which I live my life? I didn't know. I needed more help and asked Michael. He started talking about choices. I came to know that my life is my choice. Everything I think, say and do is my choice. Not my obligation, not my duty – but my choice. He told me to learn to make choices consciously and to recognize why I make them. Then see if I could make all choices from a point of peace or contentment – until I can achieve joy.

He explained that we are never victims. Wherever we are, whatever we are doing; no matter what is taking place – it is a result of our choices. This is a Truth. Our life is our choice. You may say, you never chose to be in a car accident – but your choices put you in that position. You may never have chosen to have a bad marriage – but your choices took you there. You would never have chosen to have cancer or heart disease – but your choices put you there as well. Perhaps more difficult to understand – in more out of the ordinary situations – some choices we made before we were born….but it is a Truth that everything in our life is a result of our choices. We can make the best and the most of them and be all the happier for having learned to find happiness in the moment and building upon the lessons already learned.

It is my choice what my Truth will be for this life. Everyone can have their own Truth to live by - perhaps figuring it out is the real lesson. This time they're not feeding me the answer. I must discover my one truth.

Michael talked to me about living my Truth. It wasn't until I was talking to my brother Ken one evening on the way home from work that with his help I began to have some insight into this lesson. We talked about love and we asked each other a lot of questions. Is the Truth I choose just about me or about how I interact with others? We gradually realized that our one Truth may not be the same. As we talked there were so many ideas of what the answer might be i.e. to make the world a better place through our work, to teach of light and love, to help others to name only a few.

Although there are unlimited possibilities of what my Truth could be, I kept hearing Michael asking, "What is your one Truth to live by?" I can't seem to actually "know" my one truth, but perhaps it is to honor all life. I can do this by living these lessons and continuing to learn the ten lessons. In living these lessons I know that I wish to live with love, faith, and understanding that I am connected to all living things and to all in spirit. I am learning that I am a worthy being of light – just as all living things and beings are of light. I cannot "honor" anyone with half-truths or "white lies" or by judging them for how they look, something they say or do or through anger, jealousy or hatred. It does not matter whether those around me are living their truths – it does not change that they are of light and are to be honored.

honor
Webster's 1828 Dictionary

HON'OR, v.t on'or. [L. honoro.]

1. To revere; to respect; to treat with deference and submission, and perform relative duties to.

Honor thy father and thy mother. Ex.20.

2. To reverence; to manifest the highest veneration for, in words and actions; to entertain the most exalted thoughts of; to worship; to adore.

That all men should honor the Son, even as they honor the Father. John 5.

3. To dignify; to raise to distinction or notice; to elevate in rank or station; to exalt. Men are sometimes honored with titles and offices, which they do not merit.

Thus shall it be done to the man whom the king delighteth to honor. Esth.6.

4. To glorify; to render illustrious.

I will be honored upon Pharaoh, and upon all his host. Ex.14.

5. To treat with due civility and respect in the ordinary intercourse of life. The troops honored the governor with a salute.

Somehow dwelling on honor didn't feel right to me if this lesson was about Truth. But I felt the two were connected. I asked Michael, "How can the lesson be to honor all life? I thought we were to "love" all life." He told me " You chose honor as your truth to live by. It is you who decides your truth and what shall be the focus of this life. "

The lessons are to teach and to help you heal. Love is the beginning of all the lessons. Is it not the very land upon which we are building all the lessons? Honor is to hold all life in high regard, with respect and reverence. In so doing Child, to tell untruths is not honorable, to judge another or find fault is not possible. To hurt with intent is not honor. Honor is a stepping stone to greater love."

For several weeks after I last spoke to Michael regarding truth and honor and I still didn't <u>know</u> my one truth. It felt as if I was missing something to finish this lesson. Looking for a clue or some guidance I turned to a set of "Angelic Messenger" cards by Meredith L. Young-Sowers. I spread the cards face down and randomly pulled one of the cards. Synchronistically, I pulled the card titled "Truth". In the book that accompanies the cards I read and was struck by the following sentences: "…, truth is the means through which you can honor and evaluate the meaning of your passing physical life. Truth is the acceptance of your spirit's voice and a willingness to work in whatever way is required to honor the day and to honor the Force that brings you life."

Friend, if you hadn't noticed, this is one lesson that I seemed to dance around and around and never really answered Michael's question. What is my one truth? It is in writing this several years later that I finally know the answer. I finally saw it in all their answers to my questions. Michael, my answer is: I Am Light. You Are Light. We Are All One Light.

Lesson 6

The weekend I was to hear about Lesson Six we were
expecting Hurricane Frances. The brunt of the hurricane made
land fall north of our city. We had downed trees and power
outages and everyone was asked to stay off the roads. The
neighbors were fine and there was little that could be done to
help at the moment. I began to wonder how I would get the
sixth lesson.

Since I couldn't go to the wild life refuge, I felt I was missing
my spiritual lesson. Hoping for some spiritual insight I decided
to pick an angel card from the "Angelic Messenger Cards" by
Meredith L. Young-Sowers. I fanned the cards out on the bed
face down and picked two. As I've done for years, the first
card is primary subject for review and the next a secondary
topic to study. I put the rest of the cards away and settled
down to read about the cards selected.

Just as I was about to turn the first card over I heard
Siddhartha. He told me the first card is this week's lesson. I
turned it over and the card was #12, Forgiveness. It was hard
for me to believe that this was to be how he was
communicating with me. I asked him if in the next day or so, I
could get a sign that this was really the lesson. I didn't hear
anything. I read the lesson about Forgiveness. The book that
accompanies the cards said the challenge for Forgiveness is,
"Accepting responsibility for your life; releasing blame and the
judgment of others." The book provides additional
information on Forgiveness, but I waited to hear how my guide
would teach me about this subject. As I turned the second card
over, I heard Siddhartha ask me if this would do (as a sign).
The second card was "Divine Guidance."

Sunday things were getting back to normal in our area. I went to the refuge and asked how this fit into his house metaphor. He told me the walls are to be of Forgiveness and that the walls are reinforced when Forgiveness is accompanied by an act of kindness. I wanted to know more. I asked, "Why are the walls made of Forgiveness?"

His answered with a question. "What would be kept out by having walls of Forgiveness?" Suddenly I understood. I knew that by having walls of Forgiveness I wouldn't let in anger, guilt, hate, revenge, jealousy and other similar emotions.

The way this lesson manifested in my life is the most difficult one to write about so far. Years ago one of my guides told me there are no such things as secrets. There aren't – not from those in spirit, but I won't bother to deny my desire to keep what I am about to write from those in the physical.

Not long after I heard my guides in 1993, Ken, Dr. Collins and I wanted to find out if I could hear someone who had passed. Dr. Collins agreed to let me try and speak to her Mother. At that time I knew that her Mother had passed when Dr. Collins was nine years old. She did not tell me her name. It took two attempts but I reached a lovely woman who told me her name is Helen. The first spirit I heard I believe was once close to Dr. Collins, but something about it didn't feel right. Helen did, I could feel the love in the words she was saying. I wrote Dr. Collins a note asking her, if her Mom's name was Helen and telling her I had a message for her. I can still clearly remember where I was and how stunned I felt when she told me her Mother's name was Helen and that she would like her message. Since that time I have had multiple conversations with Helen. In the years that followed, Dr. Collins has continued to teach me to grow as a person and helped me to learn about this gift. She has shared some of her life experiences to teach me. She told me how her Mother once attempted to have an abortion. This was at a time when it was impossible to have this done legally. The attempt failed. The child was not aborted and she continued to carry the baby to term. Sadly, both Helen and her baby daughter passed shortly after the child's birth due to complications that may have resulted from the attempted abortion.

Other than guides, Helen was my first conscious connection and I assumed that's why she would sometimes come and speak to me. One summer day Helen came to talk to me and naturally I thought of Dr. Collins. I was telling Helen that I don't understand why I feel an unusual connection to Dr. Collins - the way I feel toward the families of my brothers and sisters- in-law. I don't have any trouble recognizing that this is simply a client / counselor relationship. I have friends I've known for many years and that I care about very much, but this is different. Although I didn't dwell on this, it would sometimes bother me. Why did I have this strange affinity to this woman? Helen said this was easy to explain. It was because I was the baby that had died minutes after birth. I was her sister in my past life and that it was a stronger connection because it is a present life for Dr. Collins.

Being extremely skeptical about this news, it was more than a year before I told Dr. Collins what I had heard. Surprisingly, she seems to believe it. Knowing this doesn't change anything - but having told her - feeling this connection no longer bothered me. For a while I would occasionally have glimpses of her in this life - only to ask and find out that what I saw was true. One weekend I "saw" her standing under the Arch in St. Louis and later learned she was there. On another occasion I "saw" her standing in a hallway with family photos on the wall.

During this lesson of Forgiveness, Helen began talking to me while I was walking at the refuge. She said that we had something else in common and that she needed to ask me a question especially since I am learning about Forgiveness.

Helen asked me, "Could I forgive her for what she had done to me as that baby?" She wanted me to think carefully before answering. I was momentarily at a loss for words that she would ask me this question. Once I could wrap my brain around it there was no doubt the answer was yes.

I was about to cross a bridge over a canal at the refuge and Siddhartha reminded me that long ago before the lessons began another guide had referred to this bridge as the "Bridge of Forgiveness". It was when Dr. Collins and the guides were helping me to learn how to forgive myself for my own personal experience with abortion. I may have learned to forgive myself, but with all my heart I wish I had never gotten in the position to have to choose between abortion and an unknown future already filled with fear.

I realize now that Helen knew that if I answered her yes, then how could I not forgive myself as well? She was also teaching me that part of this lesson was asking for Forgiveness and in my case from the one whose life I destroyed. I had to look within again and see if I had forgiven the man who had not wanted us for a family or had not been ready to have a family then. Lastly, had I forgiven myself or simply learned to live with what I had done?

With a lot of help, I believe I have learned to forgive myself and the man who had been a part of my life for a long time. This is a painful lesson and yet thanks to Helen I know that every soul, even that of an aborted child goes on learning and there can be Forgiveness. I had to be truthful with myself and not cross the bridge until I sought Forgiveness.

How can I explain the sadness and remorse I felt as well as the awe at the possibility of re-connecting? As I had done so many times in the past, I wondered what the future might have held had I made different choices? This has been a big "What If?" in my life. When this happened I felt I was damned to hell and there could be no greater sin. How could I be forgiven for ending a life? It was against everything I had been taught and yet I made the choice. But thinking of everything I was learning on this journey and working to internalize as a way to live, I stopped, cleared my thoughts and asked for Forgiveness. Moments later I felt surrounded by love, felt the tears in my eyes and a new lightness of heart and hope.

It was in writing this that I came across a sentence I had written when Michael talked about there being a parallel universe. I wonder whether an aborted child now lives in a parallel universe or whether they have incarnated into this world to live a new life. Will someone come into my life and tell me they are this soul? I can understand how some people would say that this is an excuse or wishful thinking – a way to make choices we can't undo acceptable. Recently I asked Michael why he mentioned a parallel universe. He said, "All those who have passed still "live" and in knowing this we can understand that healing through Forgiveness allows love to flow freely again." Helen allowed me to have this opportunity, to learn what I am learning today. It could not be if not for her.

I had asked Michael to sum up the lesson on Forgiveness and this is what he said:

"Forgiveness is letting go of the fear and illusion that you and those about you are not perfect."

I had to see how this all fit and perhaps it is my understanding of the word forgive. Once more I went to my copy of the Merriam-Webster Dictionary:

Main Entry: **for·give**
1: Pardon, Absolve
2: to give up resentment of
3: to grant relief from payment of

Then I looked up the word absolve

Main Entry: **ab·solve**
1 : to set free from an obligation or the consequences of guilt
Lastly I looked up the word Pardon

Main Entry: **par·don**
1 : excuse of an offense without penalty
2 : to free from penalty

Forgiveness, I thought, is the way to end karma and come closer to God. I asked if I was on track and Michael said yes. It is only by letting go, forgiving, that we can come to realize that Forgiveness itself is an illusion – as everyone is perfect. Everyone is learning; awakening to love. We will no longer expect retribution and that the energy we set into motion is only love.

While I was preparing to write about this lesson I went to the refuge and talked with Michael about Forgiveness. He said, "When you don't forgive you close a part of yourself off. You choose what door you close." He compared it to water through a hose. We can put holes in our hose, clamp it so that the stream stops flowing all together, bend it so that there is a slight trickle. Worst of all is when we put a nozzle on it so that we might have total control. We can stop it or make it trickle, turn it into a fine shower or let it flow strongly. Recognizing our desire to control and learning to let go of the need to control our lives and the lives of others is part of the lesson of Forgiveness.

The next time I was at the refuge it was overcast and, when the wind blew, almost cool. At moments it looked like it might rain. I was standing in the lookout tower. I didn't want to be wet and cold, so I asked Michael whether I should wait out any possibility of rain and stay in the tower or head back to the car. I have asked for this information many times and always received the "correct" answer. This time it was an indirect answer to my question and he simply said, "Go." I had walked perhaps forty yards away from the tower and it started to drizzle. I wasn't really wet or even damp, but I was cold. I assumed that any second the rain was going to let loose and I was going to get soaked. I heard Michael ask, "Can you forgive me?"

There's no denying I was aggravated but I answered, "Yes, but I don't understand why you did this."

He said, "That is Forgiveness; letting go, being light without asking or knowing why."

Though I had said that I forgave him, until he reminded me again what Forgiveness really meant, I hadn't let go. It was then I also noticed that it wasn't misting anymore, the sun had come out and it was now quite warm.

Michael spoke again and asked me, "What is one of the single most important things that Dr. Collins has helped you with? It was an easy question. I knew the answer: forgiving myself. He said, "You have helped each other."

There was still more I wanted to know and I asked again, "Why are the walls Forgiveness?"

He replied, "They are of light. You will not let darkness in and on the walls of light you can hang the tapestries of your life – beautiful tapestries of your life and smaller pieces of tapestry where you have shared experiences of the lives of others.

The following week as I started upon the trail at the refuge I said good morning to everyone – Michael, my Dad, God and others. Sometimes I get singular good mornings, but usually just one big group greeting. Saturday I got a singular one, God. It was one of the longest talks I've ever had with God where I thought He was talking to me too. He asked me if I knew he had forgiven me. I said yes. He spoke of how each of us is a part of Him and that is how He experiences all that is….through the God that is each of us. He talked then of how every one of us is the sum of all our experiences and that my experiences were part of why I am writing these lessons. We are the sum of our experiences and choices. He told me that all the lessons up to this point and those to come are all interconnected. How my fear of this lesson on Forgiveness is part of Faith; Intention about what I wish to accomplish in writing this book; Unification is about how we are all connected; Evaluation has been ongoing; and without a doubt Truth has been an underlying part of this as well. He reminded me again of how there are no secrets. All is known in the Universe. Did I understand that we are so connected that the energy of every choice we make impacts the lives of others? Even my walking in the refuge this morning impacted other lives. It may become part of a statistic that determines how many people will be employed there in the future. When I purchase something in a store lives are impacted. Every choice we make: when we drive down a street, when we turn out our light to go to bed or whether we "do nothing", lives are affected by that choice too. We are all connected. My choices, my decisions will matter to others. He told me Forgiveness is about Love. Those who love also know how to forgive. "Forgiveness is an act of Love. Love is the victor over guilt, shame, hate, jealousy. Forgiveness is the seed that blossoms into Love. Was that not what my son died upon the cross?

Were those not his last words before his spirit returned to me? Those words have lasted for thousands of years to teach of Forgiveness – to teach of Love.

"Life is about learning Child. To live is to learn to Love and the choices that will bring you closer to Love. Remember Child your choices were of fear – much fear. Much fear about losing Love – a fear you still have today. Fear of judgment by others not only of you, but of your family for all that you have written. Fear of hurting those you Love and of feeling shame for the choices you have made. Are you ashamed of writing these lessons?"

I answered, "No. I think the lessons can help people."

"Many hear me in their hearts Child. You hear and feel me – my Love. I am not a God that would hurt others or you. How can I teach about Love without help? So that more may learn.

"Child, there is no death. Would I destroy what I am? The concept that energy transforms and never ends is true. I am a God of Love who lets you change all that you wish to change - your environment, your planet, your gender, your names, your shape, your partners, your work, your dreams, your life. Some may find it difficult to believe or understand but your birth was also your choice. Each of you has great strength within to call upon – the strength of God – and often you choose to test me. But it is not me that is tested, but the mind that cannot believe that we are one. It is the mind and heart that still do not recognize the one rule that was given to help all to live their lives: Treat others as you wish to be treated. Now I tell you that the walls of your home, your soul, grow stronger when there are acts of kindness and Forgiveness.

"Child, you did not always treat others as you would wish to be treated and yet that is also why you are who you are today. It is why you can understand the power of Forgiveness. It is why you are able to tell Helen yes. Because for every choice made – life changes and you have the opportunity to learn these lessons and to live by the one rule I have given to guide the lives of man. Do you understand?"

"Yes."

Lesson 7

Saturday, I had to work in the morning and then I drove directly to the wildlife refuge. When I arrived at the refuge, it was closed. I went home and went about the ordinary weekend activities. Several times throughout the day I was told to wait and Siddhartha assured me that I would get the lesson. I couldn't imagine how it might come about. I watched the remainder of a Dolphins football game, I went shopping for a while, and met a friend for dinner. We ended up talking for several hours at the restaurant. Back home I looked for a bracelet that I misplaced and while searching for it, I came across a book I had purchased six months before but never read. It is titled, "The Masters and The Path" by C.W. Leadbeater. I settled into my recliner and skimmed through the table of contents. I read paragraphs in different chapters and then I heard Siddhartha speak very softly. He said I would find the seventh lesson in this book. It would begin with the letter "P" and I would know it when I saw it. The lesson would be the doors to the house.

It took about a minute of flipping through the pages. I found it on page 54. I just felt it and knew it when I saw the words, "THE THREE DOORS". I read the poem.

> Three doors there are to the Temple
> To know, to work, to pray;
> And they who wait at the outer gate
> May enter by either way.

I kept reading the poem and the paragraph after, wanting to understand the lesson. After five or ten minutes, I asked Siddhartha what the lesson is that begins with the letter "P" and he answered, "Purpose."

When he told me the name of the lesson, all these thoughts went through my mind. We heal when we have Purpose. We find Purpose by knowing, by our work or by prayer. I thought I understood then and remembered why I first sought out Dr. Collins, because I felt I no longer had any purpose without a man in my life. I didn't know how to go on. There have been many times I have listened to people trying to find passion in their life – for their work, for another person. I believe many of us are looking for meaning in our life. I had put most of the meaning of my life into my ex's hands. What a burden for him. One of the things I always admired about him was that he always seemed to know where he was going. He knew what he wanted to be and where he wanted to live. He had his five year plan and was always working toward his goals whereas I've never known "what I wanted to be" other than successful and happy. My life is nothing like I thought it would be when I was in my early twenties.

I also thought of the times my Mother had been very down since my Father's passing. I've heard her talk of how her life no longer has any purpose at her age or in living by herself. Thankfully she seemed to get pass these times.

Remembering those moments, I began to understand the lesson. I couldn't help but wonder how this lesson would materialize in the coming days as they typically did after being introduced.

Throughout the next week I thought about the lesson and one time I heard Siddhartha tell me, "Purpose is to live each day with love; to live each day giving and receiving love."

Before I left the house for a walk at the refuge, I heard Michael asking me to be prepared to stay there a while. It was warm and humid and no one was around. I took a bottle of water and walked towards the tower. Michael talked to me and he was more specific than he had ever been before. Thursday and Friday, he had told me the outcome of two events - events that had me very worried at work and he was right both times. Things worked out satisfactorily and everything was okay as he had told me they would be.

As I walked towards the tower, I remembered that on the cover of my copy of "The Purpose Driven Life" it said, "Over twenty million copies sold". That says a lot; so many people wanting to know their Purpose in life and hoping to find answers in that book. I asked Michael to tell me more about Purpose. He asked me if I remembered what I had learned at the very beginning in the first book I ever read after that morning at the beach in 1993 when I was first aware of hearing a guide. I knew he was referring to the book, "Return to Love" by Marianne Williamson. I remembered how wonderful it felt to learn that our whole purpose on earth was to Love….to give and receive Love. If we do this - we are living a perfect life.

I still wanted to know why the lesson of Purpose has three doors. The doors are: To know, to pray and to work. He corrected this as: to know love, to pray with love and to work with love. He said that although to give and receive love is our primary Purpose, he understood that while in the physical we are all seeking to know our Purpose…our reason for being here.

He said Purpose comes through knowing, praying and working. We find joy and passion in what we do.

Often I ask to be a clear channel. He said I am a clear channel and then he told me that sometimes I would see things as I have, sometimes I would "see" in dreams and sometimes as visions. There would be times I wouldn't understand what to do with what I saw and I was to wait. Then I would know or learn the Purpose and what to do with the information I "saw". He told me I was a channel and I would be a "visionary." As he said the word visionary a hawk flew out of a nearby tree, flew a small loop and returned to the tree where it remained the whole time I was there. I often hear or see a hawk when I've been told something I may struggle to believe. He told me again how I was to teach others that there are no secrets.

Michael said things will change very quickly in my life. If I heard correctly, he said things would change by the end of the following week. Either he said this or it was wishful thinking on my part.

Then he helped me to understand what was happening at the company where I worked. I had been rather miserable that week because I couldn't find any purpose in my being there. I'm sure it was no coincidence that this was happening while I am learning the lesson of Purpose.

The one thing I feel fairly certain of is that part of my Purpose is to write down the ten lessons.

I had been at the refuge for about an hour and suddenly he told me it was time to leave. At the moment he said that I heard some rain drops on the roof of the tower and he told me not to be concerned. (I have never forgotten the time I was caught in the rain there and was so drenched by the time I got to my car it was as if I had just gotten out of a pool with all my clothes on. I had to find something in the trunk to sit on before I could even think about getting into the car.) I started walking back to my car and had gone about 40 yards when it began to rain harder….strangely while I was feeling only a little of the rain, it seemed to be coming down harder around me. It seemed like the heavens would let loose any moment so I turned around to take shelter again in the tower. I walked about 15 yards back and the rain abruptly stopped. I turned around again knowing he had told me not to be concerned. I walked those 15 yards again…and the rain drops began again. I told him I was continuing on this times no matter what happened. I walked in a very, very light rain for about 20 yards when he asked me, "What is Lesson #1?"

I said, "Faith".

He told me I was to remember the lessons we had already discussed. I didn't get wet.

The following weekend at the refuge, I still wanted Michael to explain the three doors to Purpose. There had to be more to it than I was understanding. He explained there are three doors to becoming one with God and they are through:

1) Knowing – knowing God

2) Prayer – worship, praise and petition

3) Work – experiencing good through our actions.

Knowing, I thought I understood, is that as we experience life we begin to know the wonder of God and of all that he has provided for us. We continue to learn the meaning of life – has a friend of my so aptly put - which is God as we continue each day and as we rest at night.

Prayer – often we learn about ourselves and God through prayer. How do we pray and do we listen? I believe that prayer is my way to have conversations with God and I come to my own understanding of who God is to me. I have since learned that prayer is to "ask, implore, beseech God for help, etc. Prayer is the act of asking for Divine Assistance for oneself or another."

Work – this is the most difficult one for me to understand and I'm grateful for his explanation. Michael told me I was not to confuse "work" with Career. When the guides speak of work they are not talking about my job or how I earn money. Work is when we do something to help another living entity; knowing that everything around us is energy, is life. Experiencing God through our work is finding joy and value in what we do. If we cannot find value in what we do then how shall we account for our actions to God? God wishes us to know Him, to find joy in our life, to become one with Him.

We become one with Him when we know Him, when we share our thoughts, fears, joys with Him and when our actions or activities are a celebration of life. When we are joyful we are one with God.

I asked Michael to allow me to experience example of this lesson. The following are those examples.

The first one was when I turned on the TV and "Golden Girls" was playing. In this episode the oldest character in the show, Sophia, decided to enter the convent when her friend died. She was kicked out of the convent and was telling her daughter how she was trying to find purpose in her life at this age.

The next weekend Michael talked to me while I was taking a walk at the refuge. He asked me as he had once before, "What is the Purpose of all that surrounds you at this moment? What is the Purpose of the birds, plants, animals?"

I answered, "We are all connected. All the plants and animals provide beauty and life for all. Their Purpose is to live their life to the best of their ability – to give love."

My answer was accepted and it was as if he wanted me to think of these things. He simply continued to talk about the three doors of Purpose. When I picture these three doors in my mind for some reason I am always going out the doors. I don't know why but I always think of them as exits. He told me they are entrances, gateways to realizing the Love within.

Then he spoke about Forgiveness again. He asked me to think of the house as a church for a moment. He said if the walls are Forgiveness, then once you are within those walls there is no shame, no guilt, no judgment. The only thing that existed within that church is Love.

Is it a coincidence that this past week a young man applied for a job at our company? While he had been filling out the application I recall thinking what a nice guy this is the type of guy we've been looking to hire. As he handed me his application he told me he was on parole and that he had to attend a meeting every Monday as he is a convicted sex offender. (He is required by law to disclose all this to an employer) He had served his time in prison. He told me he is not allowed to leave the state for another nine years until his probation is completed and all his family live in the northeast. I could see that it was difficult for him. There was something about him that still made me want to hire him. His sadness was visible. He seemed so resigned to being unhappy and unaccepted. He is young. I told him, I'd get back to him. I looked up his record on the local sheriff's website – where all info is available on registered sex offenders. He had been convicted twice for a sexual offense with a minor under the age of twelve. Forgiveness is a difficult subject and seems tied to trust and other emotions as well. This man was struggling to find Purpose in his life.

He asked me, "Mary, if you were to walk through each of the doors – first the door of knowing what would you find - in one sentence." I knew the door of knowing – meant knowing who

/ what I am.   But somehow I was stumbling because of all this business of Forgiveness. I kept thinking about that and things Dr. Collins told me. Perhaps we do find a way to punish ourselves and I thought about our penal systems and everything else, the stigma of various crimes, etc.

All this seemed to be going through my mind after Michael's question. I still hadn't answered him.   He said, "Mary, the walls truly are of Forgiveness and that's the only way you can look within. Let go of judgments against yourself and others so that you walk through that door knowing who you are. In that moment I felt lighter – like a small weight had been lifted from my heart and I was able to answer him. He asked me the same question for each door and this time I could answer.

He spoke then of how people are drawn to the light of a person - not unlike the bugs at night are drawn to a light.   "When you can answer the question of what you'll find when you walk through the doors of Purpose then you'll know your own light and it will shine so that it draws more light and love to it.

Several months later I bought sixty percent of the company I had been working at for the previous year. To make this acquisition I placed a significant second mortgage on my home. It was six months after the purchase that I asked Michael to give me examples of Purpose in my life. I was looking for confirmation that the purchase had been the right decision for me and I still felt as if I was missing something important in order to fully understand this lesson.

When he responded, there were so many unusual events happening that week that I filed to attach significance to the following examples, which seem obvious in hindsight.

A good friend of mine had her elderly parents staying with her for several months. Her father caught a bad case of the flu and was hospitalized. He was not rational and a bit combative with the hospital staff so she was spending as much time as possible with him, including nights to assist with his care. During this time, her mother also came down with the flu and although she was quite weak and uncomfortable, it was not as serious as her father's case. Due to her mother's age and condition, she didn't want her alone late at night while she went to spend a few hours with her father making sure he was calm and hopefully settled in. I agreed to stay with her mother. It was not a big deal for me and I was glad to be able to help.

* * * * *

The place where I work is within walking distance of a local school. During this week a boy about nine was outside our door and behaving oddly. I went to check on him and he told me he was sick. He was walking home to his grandmother's house. I offered to call his grandmother to pick him up, but he said she didn't drive and couldn't come to get him. There wasn't anyone who could come get him. I told him if he wanted to trust me, I'd drive him the few blocks home. During that short trip I found out he was hiding from bullies at school.

* * * * *

The following day a young co-worker was sick and needed a ride home. Another day I had been asked to do some energy work on someone. My mother asked me to look some things up on the internet. A friend wanted help with something on her computer. None of the requests were anything major or seemed significant; just a little odd that it was all happening at once. I still didn't see this as a lesson on Purpose and kept asking Michael to show me something.

Midway through the second week of this request, things started to go downhill at work. I tried to stay positive, keep my intentions focused. By the end of the week, I had managed only to maintain a little emotional distance from the problems. I worked at keeping it together and got through the week. Saturday morning I talked to Michael about the last two weeks and he helped me to see that part of the lesson of Purpose is to "HELP" each other. At this point I thought, "Well, I learned that lesson and everything will get back to normal."

*　*　*　*　*

A few weeks later I was on a much needed vacation with my family in New Mexico. Michael told me I would learn more about the lesson of Purpose while on that trip. It was a fun and exciting vacation. A few times I thought about this lesson and of how things were going at work. Michael reminded me then that the door called "work" is not about career. I needed to hear that. Owning a business is the most satisfying career I've had so far, but it doesn't seem to fulfill my sense of Purpose. I find it challenging but I can't say that I am passionate about what I do for a living.

What I've realized is that nothing excites me more or gives me more joy that when I learn that what I heard from my guides is true or becomes substantiated or when I can share things I've been taught by Michael and Siddhartha like these ten lessons. I had both opportunities while on vacation.

One of my three older brothers lives in Socorro, New Mexico where there is one Catholic Church and the priest's name is Father Andy. Father Andy is a sociable man of about 50 and a friend of my sister in-law and brother. Through comments by my brother and his wife, he learned that I hear things and wanted to meet me the next time I visited. While I was on vacation we had the opportunity to talk and I shared a quick summary of the ten lessons and other things with him. He also shared a little of his experiences of having been with people who are approaching death and of how they see family and friends who already departed. I also told him that when my sister in-law told me he wanted to talk, I immediately "heard" children calling out "Andy Pandy". I told him this (which is not something I would have typically done) and he told me he was called that as a boy and he had never told anyone in this town of his nickname. I had been a bit reluctant to have this kind of conversation with a priest but it turned out we both enjoyed it tremendously.

My oldest brother was quite surprised by the Priest's attitude about this and jokingly suggested that maybe he should do an exorcism on me. Father Andy responded that the Bible is filled with such occurrences as hearing things and being given messages for others. It was like being a witness to seeing seeds being planted among the others present and seeing those seeds take root.

Lesson 8

All the mental, spiritual and emotion aspects of Lesson Seven coupled with a seventy hour work week had me exhausted. I couldn't imagine that I would even hear my guide when he presented the next lesson. I'm certain it is not a coincidence that I had to work so many hours the week of Purpose.

Saturday night I was driving home from work when Siddhartha began speaking to me. He told me the eighth lesson would be the "windows". He asked me what I thought the "windows" symbolized or meant in regard to the lessons on healing.

I said, "Windows allowed light in…and out."

He said, "It is more than that."

"They allow you to see out and others to see in."

He replied, "It is more than that."

I thought a moment and if windows are symbols then it is like giving and receiving.

Again I heard, "It is more than that".

I said, "They allow you to see what is going on outside."

Once again he said, "It is more than that." Siddhartha told me to think about healing. Not knowing what to say, I went back and repeated what I had already said about light, exchanging light; giving and receiving and again I was told, "It is more than that."

This loop continued for about fifteen minutes. I wasn't making any progress.

Then he asked, "If your eyes are the windows of your soul; then what are the windows of your home? Doors allow you or others to come and go and walls keep things in or out. What of the windows?"

I asked, "Is it about clarity? Do the windows represent clarity of heart and mind - an open mind and an open heart?"

He said, "It is more than that." He told me to keep it simple and think of what the windows permit.

I don't recall whether he gave me the word or whether I finally stumbled upon it, but I said, "Sharing."

He said, "Yes. Sharing is an important part of the healing process. It is more than giving or receiving."

I asked, "How is this different than Unification?"

He answered, "It is more than that. You are all connected, but this is a conscious act of Sharing what is in your heart, mind and what is in your home. Lesson eight is Sharing."

He reminded me again of when I went to Dr. Collins the first time. I shared my thoughts and feelings and she shared her knowledge and experience to help me. He told me that all we have is only ours for a while on this earth. He went on to say that Sharing includes thoughts, feelings, emotions, material possessions, wealth, experience, knowledge, ideas, light, energy, skills and more. We are able to share all that we are and all that we possess.

Once again, this was not what I would have thought one of the lessons might be.

Later, when Michael was reviewing the lessons with me, he explained that the energy of every thought, every word and every action is shared either consciously or unconsciously. The windows we refer to are without curtains or shades. There is no need to hide as there are no secrets. He asked why would we choose to hide the light that shines within. The windows allow others to see within and for us to see from a place of light. This is truly seeing, without judgment, from a place of light and what we see, we see from Love.

Michael said, "We are light bearers." And he also spoke of triads again. The triad now is: mind, feelings, manifestations.

When I reached the tower at the refuge, we did energy work and it was more beautiful perhaps than I had ever known it to be. I sat on the steps of the tower. He told me to breathe in the light as if I were to begin channeling in Dr. Collins' office. I closed my eyes. He talked to me and told me to feel rooted to the earth and to let the energy rise within me. He spoke to me as the energy moved through each chakra and as it rose I felt more peace and filled with Love. I felt a oneness to his voice, to him and to the energy he was directing. I wanted to do healing work on my Mom and a woman named Margaret. I intended to begin with my Mother, but he directed me to Margaret. Although I do not know Margaret personally, I felt I was there with her. I felt love for this woman as I talked to her but the words seemed more theirs than mine. The words were of letting go of the fear of being hurt by others; of how she has so much strength within; of how strong the love and light is and that now she knows this strength and may heal. This strength is hers. It has been like this before but never as strong as clear. I felt energy flowing but I do not remember it moving to Margaret. We were simply one. I was then going to move on to Mom, when he instructed me to channel to Dr. Collins (to help with kidney stones) and again there was the same feeling of oneness. I was mentally talking to her too. This time the words were of how she was able to create something physical within her and of letting go of anger. She can simply love who have impacted her life and allow them to make their choices. For a few moments I could see how all our choices impact others.

One morning while walking at the refuge, Michael was unusually quiet. I had walked for quite awhile when he told me that part of healing is learning to know the love within us and for ourselves before we can share it. He told me that Sharing comes from the heart. It is not Sharing if it is perceived as a sacrifice or if we feel as if we have to do it and not because we truly want to do it. The Universe is bountiful and there is abundance for all, once we begin to heal. Twice he told me that we have to know what we are before we can know who we are.

I went for a walk at the park to see if Michael would tell me anything else to add to this lesson. He simply said that we share love, laughter, life and wisdom when others are willing to listen. He also said, "When we are Sharing our beliefs or planting seeds to help others to find or to progress along their spiritual path it is important to keep a strong foundation for our home. There are times when what is shared, is met with skepticism or not well received. Remain strong in faith and avoid judgment. Share only light."

Lesson 9

We were expecting a hurricane. It had been a busy day and I found it hard to quiet my thoughts.

Shortly after midnight that Saturday night I went to bed. I listened to the radio for awhile and then to the rattle of the shutters on the windows as the storm approached. I laid in the dark although I was wide awake. As I relaxed, I heard Siddhartha. He said, "The ninth lesson is Thanksgiving. This is the roof." This concept was so unexpected that it felt "foreign". I was struggling to understand but he didn't give me a whole lot to go on.

He told me, "In the healing process you want to get to the place where you can thank God for ALL that takes place in your life realizing that every experience is an opportunity to learn, to grow and to heal. When we begin thanking God for all the events in our lives, we'll begin to understand this and to see the events we now consider not so good in a new light." Dr. Collins has a saying "When I change my thinking and I'll change my life." It occurs to me if I can truly adapt this way of thinking, and believe in this lesson, I can never have a bad day --- and that would be healing.

I picture the house; the roof of Thanksgiving goes over the Truth, Forgiveness, Purpose and Sharing. In some ways it is the closest thing so far to God, if you imagine the structure and God sheltering us. Giving thanks as a way to heal is an entirely new way of thinking for me.

Although Siddhartha sums each of these lessons into single words, there's a lot more to them. Each time I think I completely understand the concept something happens and I find a whole new perspective that I had not contemplated before or Ken calls or emails me with his experiences and we find yet another new perspective. This was particularly true over a three day period while learning this lesson.

On Friday I met with Dr. Collins and she asked me to tell her all the things I wanted and she wrote them on an erasable board. Even in a safe and confidential environment I felt like I was revealing a secret part of myself as I listed my hopes, dreams and desires. It would seem so easy to judge someone simply by what they say they want and yet she never does that. I will admit all the wants I provided were of a personal nature. My answers were not "world peace" and afterwards I wished I had expanded my thoughts to be a bit more altruistic.

Saturday I was walking at the refuge and thinking about that list. I wanted to get back to the lessons and asked Michael about lesson nine. He asked me to think of all the things I had listed with Dr. Collins, those are things I wished to have or experience in this life. He said that I will have all of them. I didn't know what to say. I was totally lost for words. I didn't know what to think when I heard that. He continued by asking if I was thankful knowing that all this would come to me. Of course I told him. He said that is the lesson of Thanksgiving - "Being thankful knowing that God will provide all that you desire." I thought of what Dr. Collins once said, "Our thoughts are what our soul chooses to experience. Our wants and desires are part of the soul experience."

But God will provide all I desire? It's so difficult to believe, to accept.

Sunday I went back to the refuge and I was more focused. I walked for awhile and asked Michael to explain to me as simply as possible the lesson of Thanksgiving. I felt like I was still missing something important. He told me that the lesson is for each of us to learn to be thankful for God's three promises. I had never heard anyone speak of the three promises. "What are they?" I asked.

"The first is that God promises to give us unconditional love.

"The second is that there are no limits to God's love. This means that we are free to experience God, the Universe and Life in any manner we choose. We are free to experience him in any way and he will not interfere with our choices. This can include acts of great love or war and the very destruction of what he has created. We are free to learn of what we are, who we are and of Him in any way we choose.

"The third promise is that we will all come to know Him – to know God. He promises that we will learn and come to know him."

As Marianne Williamson once wrote – "Return to Love." A lot more made sense to me then.

He also told me that the triads they have spoken to me in this lesson and before the lessons were an important part of the lessons. He wanted me to include those here for people to think about.

The triads are:

Spirit

Body   Mind

Love

Energy   Trust

Manifestations

Mind   Feelings

Lesson 10

It was another Saturday morning and I was going to go get ready to go to the wild life refuge, when suddenly I knew I had to get a book from off a shelf. I actually don't know why I did it, but I did. On one shelf I have about a dozen little books, mostly White Eagle books. With only seconds of consideration I picked up White Eagle's, "Heal Thyself."

Immediately I heard Siddhartha say, I didn't need to go to the refuge to hear the tenth lesson. He said the tenth lesson is what resides within the House. It was one of those times when understanding seemed to come in a flash. It was as if several thoughts came at once and provided an immediate understanding. It wasn't that I heard sentences – I simply knew.

I understood that God resides within each of us. God is Love. Love is what fills the house. God is one with us and I am one with God. He said the tenth lesson is our affirmation and truth of this Oneness. I AM Love. It is time to live consciously as a being of love. It is a way to live with peace and gentleness.

Then I opened the White Eagle book to the last pages and it tied everything together. I found myself reading from the back forward. It tells if we focus we can feel the "ever-burning flame" and the majesty within us. We will know that we are "the masters of our body and of the conditions of our life." We will know the presence of the I AM within us and know that all things are possible. We become co-creators with God. We are aware that no matter what occurs in our life God is with us always.

Often Dr. Collins has talked to me about the difference

between Power and Force. The knowledge that this God of love is with us and we are one with him is the most amazing power within each of us. It is the power of all that is. This is a power that makes force unnecessary. Force and love do not sound symbiotic whereas love and power do.

Michael told me that lesson ten is like one of our old adages. "You really can't know someone until you live with them." He told me that was an important part of lesson ten. With lesson ten comes knowing. It is when we begin consciously living with God. The tenth lesson is to know that we are one with God. When we know that God is love, peace and gentleness we know who we are and that we are light.

He reminded me again that there are no secrets. Everything is energy. He said the ten lessons are the ten lessons of healing, the lessons of life, both our physical and spiritual life, since all is one.

As we heal ourselves we are able to sustain this oneness with God and to experience the joy of life that comes from loving all that we are and all that surrounds us. We each become channels of this love and healing power; able to heal ourselves and to help others to heal.

When he finished explaining lesson ten, Michael said, "Now Child free yourself so that you are one. Let all things flow in and out of your life without fear. Live the ten lessons – never close the doors or windows of that home and go freely through all the doors and remember that life is like a rubber band. Stay flexible and let things flow all around you, through you, and pass this on. Thank the ones that helped you to let go when you were rigid and inflexible. Thank those who gave you the pipe so that you could un-twist the band with comfort. Now live without limitations. Live knowing you are one with Love."

These are not lessons as we were presented with subjects in school where we pass one test and then move on to the next subject. These lessons overlap, grow, intertwine and have greater meaning the more they are actively experienced and consciously performed. We are continuously modifying and remodeling our homes. We are constantly changing as a physical / spiritual being. In writing this I found myself repeating some lessons even as I began to learn others. Reviewing the lessons is an ongoing process; by studying them and writing about them they have become a greater more conscious part of me. I recognize and use the lessons while living my daily life and I find myself living more joyfully. This "home" that my guides have shown me how to build is now a strong, sturdy, warm, loving place. This home is my SOUL. It is a shelter that will endure. It is the "real" or true me.

As I contemplated actually writing this book, I had an experience at Dr. Collins' office. I felt as if I actually experienced lesson ten. She used hypnosis. I only remember that she was essentially telling me that I was a good person and to look deep within myself to see who I truly am. It was one of the most amazing experiences of my life. I felt the presence and power of God within me. For about three weeks my life was changed. Fear and worry were absent from my life. I knew there was love and power within that love that would allow me to live my life fully and spiritually. I knew there was power within me to create the life I chose. There was no need for control. The power came when I let go and lived with the understanding and "knowing" that we are One with All that is and all that will ever be. While I have retained some of this – the feeling over time has faded but I know that one day it will return for good.

About the Author

The Ten Lessons were told to me several years ago over a period of ten weeks. I then spent years absorbing and comprehending them in greater depth. I've made feeble attempts over the years at writing about them. Writing has never been an activity that I particularly enjoy. Until recently, I've kept this part of my life "secret" except to Dr. Collins, a few friends and members of my family.

My story begins in St. Louis, Missouri. I grew up in a typical middle class family. I know now how hard my parents worked. I had a good childhood, fine parents and three great older brothers. My brothers and I played hard and fought often amongst ourselves. We all attended a parochial grade school, a public high school and our parents saw to it that we each received a college education.

Our childhood home was across the street from a big county park. Whenever I was upset I would take our dog or go alone and walk there. To this day, when I have things to figure out I prefer to be outside – walking. Like everyone I talked to myself about what was upsetting me. I occasionally wondered how I was able to carry on a two way conversation and do both parts. There wasn't anyone to ask and I believed it was the same for everyone. During these conversations, I only remember that I understood what had happened and I was no longer hurt or upset about the incident or angry at the person(s) involved. If I had been feeling lonely, the feeling went away. I was often surprised that by talking with myself I would come up with ideas, unexpected thoughts and solutions to my problems. It just had to be the same for everyone. Never did I think it was anything beyond my own imagination. Other times I wondered how I could know things or tell myself things that I never remembered learning. I just assumed I had forgotten who taught me.

As I child I would see "pictures" of people. There was always only one person in the photo. It could be male, female, adult or child. These pictures looked like real photographs – school photos, picture portraits or someone's snap shot. Sometimes they were black and white and other times color. I can only remember one occasion when the photo held three people and that was the night I learned what the photos meant and by that time I was in my forties. Once when I was eight or nine I was walking somewhere with my Mother when it happened. I remember asking her if she ever saw pictures of people in her head. She glanced down at me and said no. I said that sometimes I saw pictures of people in my mind. She asked me if I knew who they were. I said no and that was the end of the conversation. I went on wondering who they were. The pictures were crystal clear but only lasted two or three seconds. I have always tried to memorize the faces I saw and I would watch for these people. I never saw them and the images faded from my memory. The pictures happened every few months. It was not an everyday occurrence.

This was pretty much the same all through grade school and high school. I skipped my senior year of high school and started college six weeks after my seventeenth birthday. I attended a state college in Cape Girardeau, Missouri. I earned a B.S. in Social Work when I was twenty years old.

After several years, I found little satisfaction in doing Social Work. I took a job in sales / customer service and went to night school for a Masters in Business Administration. Once I had my degree, I took a job with a Fortune 500 company. I worked diligently and had several quick promotions. The "word" was that I was on the fast track there. It was a great company with great benefits, but I had a dream since I was a child to move to Florida. What was odd is that I had never travelled to Florida until I graduated from college and then I made two trips to Pensacola.

My childhood dream came true, when at thirty-two I moved to Florida. Although I had been seeking work in Tampa or Miami, I was hired by a company in Boca Raton. Synchronistically, this was where my high school sweetheart was living. He had moved there to attend the University for his Doctorate degree. Our relationship had been off and on again repeatedly since we were thirteen. At the time I moved to Boca Raton we were just beginning to talk again. Several months earlier we had had a nasty argument about our future while I visited him when he was living in New Jersey. It seemed we never wanted the same thing at the same time. The present was good, though we couldn't seem to agree on a future together. When it was good, it was wonderful but when it wasn't, it was usually painful for one or both of us.

Five years later, when I was thirty-seven, this relationship truly ended. I was heart-broken. This time, I hit rock bottom and couldn't seem to climb back up without help. It was seriously affecting my job. I was now Vice President of Operations at a small manufacturing company and my depression was affecting my decisions and those around me. I knew that I was in danger of losing my job if I didn't snap out of this and that just made matters worse. I knew it and I didn't know how to make myself feel better.

After close to twenty years of this on again off again relationship, my family and friends were pretty tired of hearing about it, but it was different this time. A lot had happened in the last five years and this time I knew it was over for good. I did something, I never thought I would do –I opened the phone book and called a counselor, Carol Collins, PhD.

She's an amazing woman and gifted counselor. I could write pages about how much she has taught me, how much she has helped me and how grateful I am to her. I had met with her several times. I felt better sharing it all with someone, but I was still pretty down. As I was about to leave her office, she said something like, "Mary, there is help all around you, you just have to ask." I thought she was encouraging me to pray, to ask God for help. I wasn't sleeping well and one morning at dawn I went to the beach. I was near tears again and remembered what she said and I asked (begged really) for help. Moments later I was looking around trying to find the man who was talking to me. His voice was clear and strong and he talked to me about my life and my future. He told me to tell Dr. Collins this was my "awakening" and she would know what to do. Everything he told me was beautiful and I felt so much better emotionally. A few hours later, I had a new problem: I was hearing people I couldn't see and I thought I had really gone off the deep end.

I have dreaded writing this book for years, because I have lacked faith in my ability to be able to put my story and my feelings into words. I have decided to trust in the lessons and share what I've been taught in the hope that they will be meaningful and beneficial to you.

Printed in Great Britain
by Amazon

26460045R00056